UNIV. OF MICH.

RESIDENCE OF HON. SCHUYLER COLFAX,
SPEAKER OF THE HOUSE OF REPRESENTATIVES,
SOUTH BEND, IND.

GAZETTEER

OF THE

ST. JOSEPH VALLEY,

MICHIGAN AND INDIANA,

WITH A VIEW OF ITS

HYDRAULIC AND BUSINESS CAPACITIES.

BY T. G. TURNER.

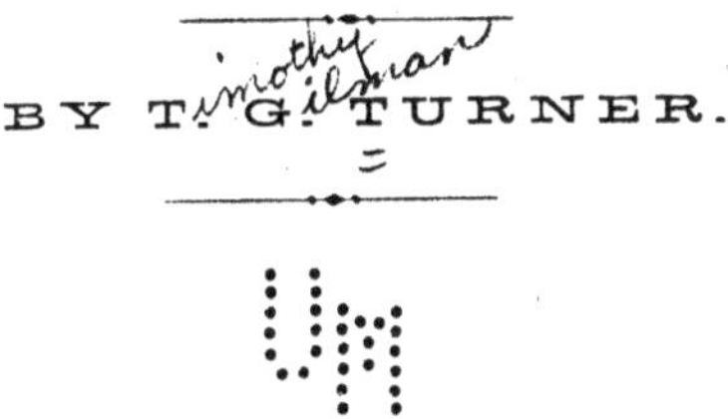

CHICAGO:
HAZLITT & REED, PRINTERS, 90 WASHINGTON ST.
1867.

F
573
.S43
T9

Entered according to Act of Congress, in the year 1867, by
T. G. TURNER,
In the Clerk's Office of the District Court for the Northern District of Illinois.

ERRATA.

Page 10, line 15 from the bottom, read " over *to* the The-au-ki-ki."

Page 13, line 19 from top, read St. Joseph Valley Railroad.

Page 28, line 11, for George "L.", read George C. Hackstaff.

Page 44, line 6 from the bottom, read *Samuel* L. Cotterell.

Page 72, at top, Joseph H. Defrees and not John D. Defrees was member of Congress.

Page 72, line 13 from bottom, for "published," read purchased.

Page 72, Alfred Hall was associated with Mr. Wheeler in the conduct of the St. Joseph Valley Register for about two years.

Page 73, line 9, for monthly read weekly.

Page 93, at top, read Nicar, Deming & Co.

Page 136, at bottom, read P. C. Perkins.

UNIV. OF MICH.

STUDEBAKER BROTHERS' CARRIAGE AND WAGON FACTORY, SOUTH BEND, IND.

THE GREAT SOUTH BEND
CARRIAGE & WAGON FACTORY

—OF—

STUDEBAKER BROS.,

A portion of which is represented on the opposite page, is located near the St. Joseph river and convenient to the Michigan Southern and Northern Indiana Railroad, eighty-five miles east of Chicago. It was established in 1852, and now ranks second to no manufactory of the kind in the West. Indiana is noted for the excellent quality of its timber—particularly the oak found upon the openings and barrens of the northern portion of the State is equal if not superior to the second growth of Connecticut and New York. This timber we use exclusively.

Attention is called to the fact that we use

SARVEN'S PATENT BUGGY WHEEL,

Which is far superior to any other known to the trade. Also,

GRANT'S SHIFTING RAIL,

By which a buggy top can be almost instantly removed, either for convenience or in case of accident.

Our wagon is known as the celebrated "South Bend Wagon," and our shop is the only one in the country where the

SLOPE SHOULDERED SPOKE

Is used. To prove our confidence in our wheels, we will give a warranty that those on our 3¼ Thimble Skein Wagon (which is best adapted to general farm use,) will carry Forty Hundred!

A branch of our house is located at St. Joseph, Mo., where can be found at all times a large and full assortment of our work, at wholesale and retail.

All classes of our wagons can also be found at the following places:

Chillicothe, Mo.............Dunn & Daily.
Kansas City, "............Plant Bros. & Co.
Little Piney, "............Fellows, McGinty & Switzler.
Hamilton, "............George Witwer.
Council Bluffs, Iowa............Wall & Hine.
DesMoines, "............Brown, Spafford & Co.
Belle Plaine, "............A. Strinagle.
Muscatine, "............R. Burtner.
Marshalltown, "............John Turner & Co.
Aurora, Ill............R. W. VanDyke.
Bement, "............John Piatt & Co.
Chattanooga, Tenn............Geo. S. Ruble.
Brenham, Texas............J. A. Trumbull.
Helena, "............John Ruckman & Bro.
Rochester, Ind............Samuel Keely.
Goshen, "............P. A. Welch.
Coldwater, Mich............B. & T. C. Etheridge.

Refer to pages 105, 113 and 126 of this book.

STUDEBAKER BROTHERS.

HISTORICAL INDEX.

Reference Books
Howgate
11-19-45
53845

GENERAL VIEW

OF THE

ST. JOSEPH VALLEY.

MUCH doubt and uncertainty hang around many of the events which go to make up the early history of a new country. The solitary wilds of an unexplored continent afford few opportunities for making those notes and records which, as time advances, become precious to the seeker after historical truths; and, as a general thing, the explorers and settlers of our Great West have been men little accustomed to literary pursuits and less desirous of literary honors. Besides, the arduous labors and engrossing duties of pioneer life leave little room or opportunity for that quiet and leisure indispensable to scholarly habits. Thus it is, that a considerable portion of the interesting events of our first settlements, and of the discovery of the country itself, have faded from the memory of man or are only handed down as traditions, distorted by the uncertain medium or mystified by the lapse of time. True, occasionally men of learning and taste have wandered into the very heart of the continent and, with fertile pens, have recorded what they did, and saw and suffered. Especially is this true of those adventurous French explorers who first penetrated the unbroken forests and traversed the almost boundless prairies of the West; yet, even they left much for doubt and more for conjecture. Their relations are frequently little more than skeletons around

0 12-5-45 L.H.

which the busy imaginations of subsequent writers have moulded forms to suit their purposes or to please their fancies. It is not, therefore, strange that the time of the discovery and the identity of the discoverer of the river and valley which form the subject of this brief sketch are matters of dispute. To be sure, this may be said to be a circumstance of not much practical importance, but it is a source of regret to the enterprising investigator. The French explorer LaSalle has generally been accredited the honor of this discovery. The Griffin, a vessel of sixty tons, was launched by him on Niagara river, in 1679, and in her, accompanied by over thirty men, he sailed on the seventh of August of that year, bound for the valley of the Mississippi. He crossed lakes Erie and St. Clair and arrived at Green Bay, September second. The Griffin was the first vessel which ever navigated these lakes. She was wrecked on her return trip.

Coasting along the east shore of lake Michigan, with Hennepin, Tonti and some thirty followers, on the first day of November, 1679, he came to the St. Joseph, which he then called the Miamis, or the "River of the Miamis," from the name of an Indian tribe living upon it. Here he built a fort. A recent writer professing to draw his facts from reputable sources, supposes the site of this fort to have been Chicago, and the Miamis the Chicago river, a most preposterous supposition when all authentic accounts agree that from this fort LaSalle started on the third of December with twenty-three men and came up the St. Joseph to the portage near South Bend, and passing over the The-au-ki-ki or Kankakee, went down that river to the Illinois. The site of his fort is still pointed out at St. Joseph; and the remains of another built by him ont the river near Niles, Michigan, is still to be seen. There is no doubt but LaSalle discovered the *mouth* of the river, and was the first voyager upon it for seventy miles towards its source.

In 1673, Frontenac and Talon, the governor and intendant of Canada, resolved to send an expedition, under Louis Joliet, to explore the direction and mouth of the Mississippi. Father Marquette was directed to accompany the party as missionary. During this expedition, and probably in the latter part of the summer of 1673, it is said Marquette passed up the Illinois and Kankakee rivers and over the portage to the St. Joseph of the lakes. If this be so, of which there seems to be no doubt, then his was the first European eye that ever rested upon the waters of this lovely river, and that too, at a point not two miles distant from the present city of South Bend. This was more than six years before the discovery of LaSalle. A narrative of Marquette's voyage, first published in 1681, and also of a journal of his last expedition, with autograph maps, may be found in Shea's "Discovery and Exploration of the Mississippi Valley." The doubts once entertained of the authenticity of these papers no longer remain.

These conflicting claims are briefly stated here rather incidently, but not with a view to discuss them, nor to make any determination of the issue. As we have before said, the matter is of no great practical importance—no greater, perhaps, than it would be to know for a certainty whether the continent of America was first discovered by Biorn of Iceland, Leif the son of Eric the Red, or by Columbus the Genoese. The curious may settle it if they can.

The valley at the time of its discovery, was occupied by Indians, mostly of the Potawattomie tribe, interspersed by a few Miamis and Chippewas. It was a favorite resort for those "red men of the forest," and remains of some of their villages and cornfields are said to be found at the present time. Some of these settlements were as follows: Chebass', Casson's and Topennebee villages, near Niles, Musconginon, Weesaw, Pokagon, Mishawaka and Mongonghanon.

In 1828, Gen. Lewis Cass, then Territorial Governor of the State of Michigan, made a treaty at the Mission near Niles, by which the Indians ceded to the United States all their lands in the valley with the exception of some small reservations. A few years afterwards these reservations were also ceded to the Government, and in 1840 about two thousand of the aborigines under the conduct of Alexis Coquillard, left for their new home west of the Mississippi. In 1843, Mr. Coquillard removed all the remaining Indians, leaving the white man in full and undisputed possession of their ancient territory. The removal was entirely voluntary on the part of the Indians. They had the option presented to go in peace or by the gentle persuasion of the bayonet. Deeply sensible of the law of necessity which applied to their case, by an extraordinary effort of free will, they voluntarily departed!

Previous to 1830 the only means of access to the valley was by two Indian trails, one from Detroit and the other from Fort Wayne, intersecting at Niles; and by coasting along lake Michigan to the mouth of the river. Soon after that date, the Territorial road from Detroit to Chicago, the Vistula road from Toledo to South Bend, the Michigan road from Madison to Michigan City and the State road from Fort Wayne to South Bend were opened and an impetus thereby given to immigration. At the present time it is penetrated by two of the most important trunk lines of railroad to be found on the continent. The Michigan Central was the first railroad built in the State whose name it bears. Its beneficial effect throughout the region which borders upon it have been very great. It runs from Detroit through the beautiful towns of Ypsilanti, Ann Arbor, Jackson, Marshall, Battle Creek and Kalamazoo to Niles; thence through Buchanan and Michigan City to Chicago; making a total distance of two hundred and eighty-four miles. It was commenced and partially built by the State at a time when financial Dogberries ruled her legislative destinies; but in 1844 it passed into the hands of the present corporation, and was soon completed and ready for business. It has been well and successfully managed; in proof of which reference need only to be made to its universal popularity along its entire route and with the public generally.

The Michigan Southern and Northern Indiana railroad was completed to South Bend in the month of November, 1851, and soon after was opened from lake Erie to lake Michigan. It runs through the Valley of St. Joseph from near Hillsdale, in Michigan, to the western part of St. Joseph county, Indiana. It is entirely impossible to estimate the material advantages derived from this mammoth line of communication, by all the territory which it traverses. By it, South Bend is one hundred and fifty-seven miles from Toledo and eighty-five from Chicago. It is one of the best constructed railroads in the United States, and its management is unexceptionable in every respect. Its capital stock is $10,601,200, and its bonded debt $9,135,840, making the aggregate capital invested nearly $20,000,000. Its gross earnings for the year ending February 28th, 1867, were $4,673,129.86. During the same year the total number of miles run, by all kinds of trains, was 2,386,193, or more than ninety-five times around the globe! The track owned, maintained and operated by this company, is as follows:

Toledo to Chicago, old line	242.06 miles.
Main track north of 22d street, Chicago	1.18 "
Toledo to Elkhart, air line	133.20 "
Air Line Junction to Detroit	61.51 "
Adrian to Monroe Junction	33.60 "
Palmyra Junction to Jackson	44.40 "
Side tracks	62.32 "
Total	578.27 "

There are only seven hundred and sixty-eight feet of wooden bridging upon the road, and this will soon be replaced by permanent structures of stone.

It is worthy of especial remark, that during the year, the amount received for way passengers exceeds the amount from through passengers by $271,319, a fact not only showing the character of the country through which it runs, but suggestive to the managers of the importance of cultivating this branch of traffic. E. B. Phillips, Esq., is President, and Chas. F. Hatch, Esq., General Superintendent.

The St. Joseph railroad runs from White Pigeon, on the Michigan Southern and Northern Indiana road, by way of Constantine, Three Rivers and Schoolcraft to Kalamazoo, a distance of about thirty miles. This road, as far as Three Rivers, was built and for several years operated by the Michigan Southern and Northern Indiana Company. The whole road is now under the management of Ransom Gardner, Esq., and is an important line of communication and traffic for a large and fertile portion of the valley.

A railroad is now in process of construction from Port Huron, in Michigan, by the way of Flint, Lansing and Battle Creek, Michigan, and Mishawaka to South Bend. It is called the "Peninsular," and is intended to be a first class road in every respect. From South Bend it will be carried forward to Chicago, by the way of Laporte and Valparaiso, so that the connection between the termini will be continuous and complete. The whole length of this route is about three hundred and twenty-nine miles, viz.: from Port Huron to Flint, sixty-five miles; from Flint to Lansing, forty-five miles; from Lansing to Battle Creek, forty-five miles; from Battle Creek to Indiana State Line, sixty-nine miles; from State Line to Chicago, one hundred and five miles. A large proportion of the road bed, in the State of Michigan, is already graded; and at least that portion between Port Huron and Flint will be ironed and in perfect running order before the close of 1867. Arrangements have been made for the necessary material aid, so that the early completion of the Peninsular road is placed beyond a peradventure or a doubt.

Enterprising capitalists are moving with a view to the construction of a railroad from the mouth of the St. Joseph river, by the way of Berrien and Niles, in Michigan, to South Bend and thence to intersect the Chicago and Peru road at Plymouth. The distance is about sixty miles; and the road when built will doubtless be a very important and profitable one. Both these contemplated roads will be of great advantage in developing the resources of the country through which they will pass.

The St. Joseph takes its rise in a small lake, called Baw-Beese, in Hillsdale county, Michigan, near the county seat, and runs thence north-west into Calhoun county. Near Tekonsha it makes an abrupt bend, and its general course thence to South Bend is south-westerly. From South Bend to Lake Michigan it runs nearly north. From its head to its mouth the river flows through a rich, level and well cultivated country, and neither upon or near any of its numerous tributaries can be found a mountain nor many elevations that aspire to the dignity of hills. The face of the valley is undulating, sometimes quite rolling, but everywhere well adapted to purposes of husbandry. The landscape is beautified by many small lakes and brooklets, and occasionally unimportant marshes are found; but these last are fast disappearing under a uniform and general system of drainage. The source of the river is on the ridge dividing the waters of lake Erie from those of lake Michigan, and which is, perhaps, the highest point of land on the Peninsula. The descent from Hillsdale to lake Michigan is gradual but constant and considerable, so that the St. Joseph, although flowing through a remarkably level country has, at almost every point, a rapid current. Being fed largely from springs and lakes, it is not subject to rapid and excessive rises nor to inconveniently low stages of water. Inundations are infrequent and unimportant. Its chief tributaries are the Coldwater, Fawn, Pigeon, Little Elkhart, Elkhart, Dowagiac and Paw Paw rivers, all of which are valuable mill streams.

Unlike all mountain streams, the St. Joseph, instead of decreasing in its volume as the surrounding country is cleared and improved, has exhibited a very decided increase. This is caused by the drainage of marshes and low lands, thus bringing into the current of the river a large quantity of water which was heretofore spread over a vast area and there been left to evaporate to the detriment of health and to the general damage and discomfort of the country. This accretion is constantly going on and for many years must add very materially to the volume of the stream. A steamboat called the Schuyler Colfax, of about two hundred tons burthen, is now plying regularly between South Bend and the mouth of the river, meeting with little or no obstruction, even at the present low stage of the water. For years much of the commerce of this valley was carried on by steam and keel boats quite successfully. It now only requires a comparatively small outlay of means to complete slack water navigation as far up as Three Rivers, in Michigan. A few locks and dams only are needed to perfect the navigation for steamers of three hundred tons burthen. Such an improvement would be highly advantageous to those whose business involves the moving of heavy and bulky freight.

But a little more than thirty years have elapsed since emigration was fairly directed towards this valley. Then, there were no roads, no houses, no mills, no improvements of any kind. Supplies had to be brought from a distance, and at great expense and hazard. The sickness, suffering, privation and discouragement incident to all new settlements in the West, had to be encountered. Homes had to be made, society formed and all the appliances of civilized life to be wrought out by courage, perseverance and industry. The pioneers of the valley and their successors have done nobly. Few sections in all the Great West can show equal results. The contrast and the progress made will more fully appear by the following figures:

The amount of flour received at Toledo by the Michigan Southern and Northern Indiana Railroad for the years indicated and from the places named, all being properly included in the Valley of St. Joseph, is as follows:

	1864. NO. BBLS.	1865. NO. BBLS.	1866. NO. BBLS.
South Bend	30,834	38,954	21,741
Mishawaka	6,786	30,436	11,935
Elkhart	19,419	31,438	22,551
Bristol	10,097	12,834	8,328
Middlebury	2,194	4,008	2,089
Three Rivers	3,300	28,757	31,130
Constantine	17,828	24,526	12,126
White Pigeon	8,208	11,346	5,803
Sturgis	8,378	14,310	6,000
Burr Oak	3,908	9,242	5,100
Bronson	485	888	164
Coldwater	11,706	17,303	5,321
Quincy	938	200	3,432
Jonesville	7,165	10,046	1,026
Goshen	24,628	31,880	16,195
Total	155,874	266,162	152,941

The amount of grain received, as above, for the same years, was, in 1864, 725,238 bushels; in 1865 it was 770,075 bushels; in 1866 it was 447,878 bushels. The almost total failure of the wheat crop and the short corn crop of 1866 is the cause of the falling off in that year. The year 1867 will undoubtedly show a greater export of flour and grain from the places named above than was ever known in a former year, by the equivalent of more than half a million bushels. The figures already given, of course, do not include the quantities sent west and that shipped by the lake and by the Michigan Central Railroad.

The fruit exports including apples, peaches, strawberries, huckleberries and cranberries, are almost incredible, but we have no means of giving even a proximate of the actual amount. In one week the present summer, over seven thousand bushels of strawberries were sent to Chicago, from the port of St. Joseph alone. The peach crop along the lower valley, is of very great value and is seldom known to be a failure.

The population of the Valley, as shown by the census of 1860, aggregates as follows:

In Michigan	131,045
In Indiana	50.113
Total	181,158

An estimate for the present time, founded upon the ascertained rate of increase, gives 287,684. This includes six counties and half of five others.

To say that the St. Joseph river is a beautiful stream of water and that the country through which it flows is a very pleasant and productive valley of land would be a truthful generalization not likely to be disputed, but equally applicable to many other rivers and their surroundings. Indeed, it may be doubted whether the eye of the poet or of the painter would here meet with that satisfaction easily to be found in more ungenial climes and amid more rugged formations. To the eye of the utilitarian, however, he who seeks for more immediate and more practical uses, very little is here wanting to insure the highest gratification. Almost from its very source, the river has such a volume of water and such a gradual but decided fall, as to afford a succession of valuable locations for the development of hydraulic power; and the country which it at once waters and drains, though in many places highly picturesque and beautiful, is noted more than for all else, as a section where rural abundance is almost spontaneous. Perhaps no valley in the land, of equal size, is capable of yielding more sure or more ample rewards to the industrious worker, or offers greater facilities for the support of a dense population of enterprising people. This fact cannot but be apparent to even the casual observer. The numerous and large fields of all the cereals adapted to the latitude bear ample testimony to the quality of the soil; natural meadows, thickly set in the rich native grasses and affording abundant and excellent herbage; orchards laden with their pomological treasures, gladdening the sight and tempting the appetite; gardens rejoicing in succulent luxuriance; natural forests of useful and ornamental trees, all these and much more, give to the landscape an air not only of plenty but of absolute profusion. Add to all this the fact of easy culture, speedy and cheap transportation and a good and never failing market, and the dream of the agricultural utopian appears to be realized. But add, further, the extraordinary facilities for all manner of industrial pursuits afforded by the immense hydraulic power of the river, and a reality, not a picture, is produced which challenges competition or comparison.

Each town and village along the valley, which has struggled up from the days of the early settlement of the country, is now becoming the nucleus of a thriving and important center of industry and trade. The rose colored expectations of the first settlers and the feverish excitement occasioned by the construction of railroads through the country, each visionary and delusive, have subsided into a more sober and practical view of things, and now there seems to be not only a rational appreciation of the facilities which nature has afforded, but a substantial exhibition of that practical application and energetic action which form a sure presage of success. A generation of white men have quietly seen the St. Joseph river sweeping past their doors, wasting its mighty powers in improvising sand-bars and in dancing over riffles. That generation, while waiting, like Micawber, for "something to turn up" to their advantage, have passed away. A new era has dawned. Enterprise is at work. Genius and art; intelligence and thrift; capital and labor have combined in a sort of co-operative union for the purpose of subjecting to humanizing uses the hitherto unappropriated and unappreciated capabilities of the situation.

HILLSDALE COUNTY, MICHIGAN.

This county, containing some of the highest land in the Peninsula, is the fruitful mother of rivers. Here rise the St. Joseph of Lake Michigan, the St. Joseph of the Maumee, the Raisin and the Kalamazoo. Several other small streams rise in, or traverse the county. The surface is generally rolling, with abrupt swells, which may, perhaps, properly be called hills. The soil is rich and productive. In several places fine quarries of a very good quality of sand stone crop out, well adapted for building—almost the only ones to be found in the lower peninsula. Lime and iron ore are found, though not in large quantities. Wheat, corn, potatoes and wool are the chief agricultural productions. The village of HILLSDALE is the county seat. It is very pleasantly situated near the outlet of Baw Beese lake, and is noted for the romantic beauty of its surroundings. It enjoys a large and increasing trade, and its manufactures are in a thriving condition. Hillsdale College, a large and esteemed institution, under the control of the Freewill Baptists, is located here. Both male and female students are admitted.

The village of JONESVILLE is situated about four miles northwest of Hillsdale, on the Michigan Southern and Northern Indiana Railroad and on the St. Joseph river, which even here, furnishes a very good water power. It is, properly, the first village in the valley descending the river. Its population is estimated at nearly two thousand, who are noted for intelligence and enterprise. It contains several manufactories, among which is an extensive woolen factory.

CALHOUN COUNTY, MICHIGAN.

This is one of the finest counties in the State, and contains seven hundred and twenty square miles. The soil is mostly a rich sandy loam, with some black alluvial loam in the river bottoms. It is one of the chief wool producing counties in Michigan. The population in 1860 was 29,398. It is noted for its superior public schools. In 1860 there were 7,968 children attending school. There were 116 male and 212 qualified female teachers, to whom was paid $22,258.40. It has two flourishing cities, Marshall, the county seat, and Battle Creek, both situated on the Central railroad and the Kalamazoo river, and some thirteen miles apart. The population of the former in 1860 was 4,000 and of the latter about the same. The village of Tekonsha is situated near the St. Joseph river, on the stage route from Coldwater to Marshall. It has a good water power and is a thriving town. Ten miles below Tekonsha is the village of Burlington, also on the St. Joseph, and containing some three hundred people. It is fourteen miles north of the Michigan Southern and sixteen miles south of the Central railroad. It has some manufactories, including a machine shop.

BRANCH COUNTY, MICHIGAN.

From its source, the St. Joseph river runs nearly north-west into Calhoun county, after which brief diversion it turns south-westerly, and after touching the county of Branch, goes no farther north again than the southern tier of counties in Michigan. It makes a detour into Indiana but, returning very suddenly, pursues its course with great rapidity to its native State and empties its treasure of waters into Lake Michigan not more than five miles from a due west line from its source. At Union City, in Branch county, the Coldwater river debouches into the St. Joseph, thus making the whole county tributary to and a part of the valley.

The county of Branch in point of location, fertility and general advantages, is hardly surpassed by any other county in the peninsular State. It was organized in 1833, having been previous to that time a part of St. Joseph county. It contains five hundred and twenty-eight square miles. In 1860 it had a population of 20,981, and has now at least 30,000. The estimated value of its real and personal estate is over twelve millions of dollars. The surface is generally level and the soil diversified, but all of it producing crops of extraordinary abundance. It is watered by the St. Joseph, Big Swan, Little Swan, Prairie and Coldwater rivers and numerous small creeks and rivulets which become tributaries to the larger streams. The Michigan Southern and Northern Indiana railroad passes through the county and has been a source of inestimable benefit to it. J. B. Crippen, Esq., formerly an enterprising citizen of Coldwater, a few years since published a *Monthly Journal* at that place, from which the following is extracted:

"When this county constituted a part of St. Joseph, it was known as the township of Green. Afterwards the towns of Coldwater and Prairie River were organised; the former embracing the eastern, the latter the western portion of the county. From time to time other towns were organized; the names of some have been changed, and now we have sixteen. The county seat was first located in 1831, at Masonville, on the east branch of the Coldwater river, by commissioners appointed for that purpose. But their location not being confirmed, it was removed in October of the same year to Branch, a few miles south-west of there, within the township of Coldwater. * * * * * * In 1842 the county seat was removed by an act of the legislature to the village (now city) of Coldwater.

"The settlements in this county were commenced as early as 1828. The trials and difficulties which the pioneers had to endure and contend with were many, among which, not the least was the want of mills. There was no mill for grinding grain nearer than Constantine, thirty-five miles west, or Tecumseh, fifty-five miles east, and it was a journey of several days to and from either of those places, traveling by marked trees through the woods.

"In 1829, Messrs. Foster and LeRonge had an Indian trading house, west of the Coldwater river, on the north side of the Chicago road. Mr. Godfroy had a trading house at the east end of Coldwater Prairie; and afterwards Lorin Marsh established a trading house on the west bank of the river, on the south side of the Chicago road. Mr. Bonner, a Welchman, was the first white man who came with his family to the township of Coldwater. Rev. E. H. Pilcher preached the first sermon on Coldwater Prairie, and also conducted the first funeral exercises, on the occasion of the death of a child of Allen Tibbits. Rev. Allen Tibbits was the first resident preacher of the gospel. He emigrated to this country in 1831, and delivered his first discourse in July of that year. Wales Adams came from Massachusetts, and located in the western part of the county, in the year 1830, where he erected one of the first saw mills built in the county, on a stream called Prairie river." Allen Tibbits, spoken of in the above extract, still lives at Coldwater. He long since abandoned the clerical profession, and is now a respectable citizen and an alderman of that thriving city.

The city of COLDWATER, the seat of justice of Branch county, is situated on the east branch of the river of the same name, and not far from Coldwater lake. Mr. Clark, in his Gazetteer of Michigan, says that "this is one of the most beautiful and pleasantly located towns in the country, being located in the center of a farming region that is unsurpassed for fertility and productiveness, and inhabited by an enterprising and refined class of people, who evidently take great pride in rendering their city neat and attractive." It has a population of over five thousand, and is distinguished for the intelligence of its women and the beauty of its men.* It sent many good soldiers to the late war, furnished material for three or four generals, and was worthily represented in the quartermaster's department. The celebrated Loomis' Battery went from here, and the six guns with which they did such splendid service have been returned to the city, and are there held as mementoes of patriotism and valor. Aside from the elegant public school, built at a cost of over $30,000, the public buildings are unimportant. The court house is far from modern in its arrangements and much too small. The jail is a disgrace to modern or any other kind of civilization; indeed, it is not equal, in size, style and comfort, to a majority of the stables in the city. If common humanity does not soon prompt the building of a new and better one it is to be hoped that some sense of shame will. It may be remarked that the people of the city, as a general thing, see and deplore this blot which the inhabitants of the "rural districts" seem determined to perpetuate. There is located here a very fine "Young Ladies' Seminary" which is performing a work of great usefulness.

The first white settlement was made in 1829, by a man named Campbell. On the 30th of October, of the same year, the eldest daughter of Mr. Allen Tibbits died, and she was the first white person buried in the town. In 1832, the village was laid out by Joseph Hanchett and Allen Tibbits, and was called Lyons. The following year the name was changed to Coldwater, that being the interpretation of Chuck-sen-ya-bish, the Indian name of the neighboring river. The first meeting house was erected in 1836.

---

* Vide the Mistletoe Bough.

An organization under a city charter was effected in 1861, when Albert Chandler was elected the first Mayor.

The first newspaper issued in Branch county was published in the village of Branch, then the county seat, in 1832, and was called the *Michigan Argus*. In 1833 Dr. Calkins issued the *Coldwater Observer*, in the village of Coldwater. In 1842 the *Observer* passed into the hands of M. B. Josselyn, who changed the name to *Coldwater Democrat*, and published it till 1844, when Albert Chandler purchased it and continued it some five years, at the end of which time it was discontinued. It was born, lived and died a Democrat. The *Branch County Journal* was started in November, 1851, by B. F. Thompson, and in 1856 it passed into the hands of Eddy, Gray & Co., who changed the name to *Branch County Republican*. In 1862 the *Republican* was bought by Franc B. Way and changed to the *Branch County Gazette*. This paper has been Republican throughout, and is now published by Benton & Burr.

The *Democratic Union* was commenced by the late Captain John L. Hackstaff, in 1856, and continued until 1861, when its publisher and editor, at the call of his country, went into the army, from which he returned only to die of disease contracted in the service. The *Southern Michigan News*, an independent paper, was started in March, 1862, under the editorial charge of T. G. Turner, and was discontinued in the following winter, when the editor went into the army. The *Welcome Guest*, a Spiritual paper, was published for several months in 1859, by Loudon and Hackstaff; and James B. Crippen, Esq., in 1861, issued an advertising sheet called *Crippen's Monthly Journal*, evincing considerable editorial ability. In 1864 Frederick V. Smith commenced the *Coldwater Sentinel*, at first an independent paper, but now of the Democratic faith. It is still published by Smith and Moore, and ably edited by the former gentleman. The *Republican*, the politics of which is denoted by its name, was commenced in the summer of 1866, by Major D. J. Easton, and is now published by W. J. & O. A. Bowen. It is a quarto sheet of very fine appearance, and may fairly claim to be a first-class weekly newspaper.

QUINCY is an incorporated village, on the Michigan Southern Railroad, six miles east of Coldwater. It is a place of considerable trade, and has about twelve hundred inhabitants.

The village of BRONSON is twelve miles west of Coldwater, and has a population of some five hundred. It is a brisk little town, and has recently been contesting with its proud neighbor, the honor of being the county seat. As yet it has been unsuccessful.

UNION CITY is a pleasant town, at the mouth of the Coldwater river, twelve miles northwesterly from the county seat, and on the St. Joseph. It has a fine water power, as yet unimproved, except on the Coldwater. Had it a railroad connection with the rest of the world, it would soon equal if not surpass any town in the county.

3

ST. JOSEPH COUNTY, MICHIGAN.

In point of fertility of soil and general natural advantages, St. Joseph is among the foremost counties in the valley. One of the peculiarities of this county is thus related by Mr. Clark: "In various parts of this and the adjoining counties are found interesting traces of a species of agriculture practiced by a race that inhabited this region at some very remote period. These remains are in the shape of ancient garden beds, laid out with mathematical precision, and occupying, oftentimes, a great extent of ground, frequently covering from one to three hundred acres in a single field or garden. They are generally found in prairies or burr oak plains. They appear in fanciful shapes, but order and symmetry of proportion seem to govern. Some are laid off in rectilineal or curvilineal figures, either distinct or combined in a fantastic manner, in parterres and scolloped work, with alleys between, and apparently ample walks or avenues, leading in different directions, displaying a taste that would not discredit a modern pleasure garden. On the west bank of the St. Joseph river, a short distance from the village of Three Rivers, a garden of this kind is still to be seen in tolerable preservation. The garden is judged to be half a mile in length by one-third in breadth, and contains upwards of one hundred acres, regularly laid out in beds, running north and south, in the form of parallelograms, five feet wide, one hundred feet long, and eighteen inches deep, with alleys between them eighteen inches wide and eighteen inches deep. At the extremity of each is a semi-lunar bed, or semi-circle, of the same depth and diameter, corresponding to the width of the beds. The beds have the appearance of being raised above the surrounding country, and are as regular and distinct as if but recently made. One of the most singular circumstances connected with these remains is that the Indians of the neighborhood were evidently in perfect ignorance of their originators or their uses. * * * * It is evident that these gardens were constructed and cultivated by a race of men in every way superior in intelligence and civilization to the American Indians of the present or past century."

This county had in 1860 an aggregate population of 21,111. At the present time it probably has about 31,500. There are several incorporated villages in the county. Descending the St. Joseph river, the first is COLON, with a population of about six hundred, and six miles below, MENDON, of about the same size. Both of these towns have good, but undeveloped, water power in abundance.

The flourishing and enterprising village of THREE RIVERS is situated at the confluence of the Portage river and Rocky creek with the St. Joseph, whence the name. The St. Joseph Railroad runs through, connecting it with both the Michigan Southern, at White Pigeon, and the Central, at Kalamazoo, it being twelve miles to the former and eighteen to the latter place. The population is estimated at about 2,500. Three Rivers is at the head of navigation on the St. Joseph. To this point, for many years before the completion of the great east and west railroads, steamers of light draught constantly plied from Lake Michigan, Lockport, Brooklyn and Canada, three adjoining settlements, are regarded as suburbs of Three Rivers. The hydraulic power afforded by the three streams which here mingle their waters is immense, and unsurpassed in the State, except at Grand Rapids. It is improved to some extent, but there is still a large surplus awaiting the demands of capital and enterprise.

The first settler was Jacob McEutenfer, in 1830. The village was laid out in 1836, and incorporated in 1857. The first church was erected in 1838.

At the point where Fawn river falls into the St. Joseph, and on the railroad from White Pigeon to Kalamazoo, four miles from the Michigan Southern road, is situated the village of CONSTANTINE, with something over fifteen hundred inhabitants. Fawn river furnishes a first class water power, which has been liberally improved and profitably used. The St. Joseph has never been dammed here, but offers great inducement for such an improvement. The town is handsomely laid out, and is ornamented with a good degree of taste. It is one of the most beautiful and live towns of the West, and is worthy the particular notice of those who are seeking locations for business.

White Pigeon is located on the Southern Michigan and Northern Indiana Railroad, near the Indiana line, and is the Southern terminus of the St. Joseph road. Pigeon river flows through the town, and affords good and abundant water power. Considerable manufacturing is done here, and the town is in a healthy and flourishing condition. The population is nearly or quite two thousand. A very good newspaper is published here, called the *Democratic Union*, by George L. Hackstaff & Co. The "office" is the same one used by Captain Hackstaff, now deceased, in printing his paper of the same name at Coldwater, several years ago.

Twelve miles east of White Pigeon, on the railroad, in the midst of one of the finest prairies in the West, is the village of Sturgis, with a population of nearly two thousand. It is a thriving town, and likely to become a prominent point on the Michigan and Indiana Railroad, which is now being built and which will here cross the Michigan Southern. It has one newspaper, the *Sturgis Journal*, edited by Hon. J. G. Wait.

Burr Oak is six miles to the east of Sturgis, and has about eight hundred inhabitants. The village is prosperous.

Centerville is the county seat of St. Joseph, and is tastefully laid out, in the interior of the county. It has several fine residences and respectable county buildings. The Prairie river furnishes a fair water power which is improved to some extent. The sound of the locomotive never echoed through the streets of Centerville, and as a consequence it has only about six or seven hundred people.

Returning to the St. Joseph river, we come to Mottville, a few miles below Constantine. Settlements and considerable improvements were made here at an early day. It has a splendid water power but no railroad communication. General Hart L. Stewart, now of Chicago, was one of the first settlers here, and was formerly a large landholder, and one of the most enterprising men in the county. Better days may be in store for Mottville. It needs only enterprise and industry to raise the population far above eight hundred, which is about the present number. We now pass into Indiana.

ELKHART COUNTY, INDIANA.

This county is bounded north by the State of Michigan, east by Noble and LaGrange counties, south by Kosciusko county, and west by St. Joseph county. It is divided into sixteen townships, viz.: Cleveland, Baugo, Olive, Locke, Osolo, Concord, Harrison, Union, Washington, Jefferson, Elkhart, Jackson, York, Middlebury, Clinton and Benton. Its aggregate population at the present time does not vary much from 30,000. In 1860 it was, according to the census returns for that year, 20,986, showing an increase in seven years of at least 9,014. Assuming this as the rate of increase for the ten years ending in 1870, the number at that date will be near 35,000, which will be found to be under rather than over the mark. The first census was taken in 1830, for which the county paid the sum of four dollars and fifty cents, a fact warranting the inference, perhaps, that the number of inhabitants was not large, although what it was does not appear.

The county was organized in June, 1830, by James Matthews, John Jackson and Armenius C. Penwell, constituting the Board of Justices, the former of whom was elected president. At a special meeting of the board, in the following July, all the territory in the State east of the present limits of the county was erected into a township, and called Mong-go-qua-nong. The territory constituting this township of magnificent proportions and distances, as well as name, was attached to Elkhart county for judicial and other purposes, and has since been organized into several counties. The territory now forming a part of Kosciusko county, on the south, was also attached to Elkhart at that time, and was known as Turkey Creek township.

In May, 1830, the commissioners appointed under the organizing act of the Legislature, located the county seat on the southwest quarter of section twenty-four, in Concord township; but in 1831 this location was changed, and the seat of justice was finally established at Goshen, where it still remains. Here the first court of record was held, by the associate judges of the county, in November, 1830, who were allowed and paid for their judicial services, in addition to the honor which they enjoyed, the sum of four dollars each.

In July, 1830, the first merchant's license was issued to Dominique Rouseau, an Indian trader of those times.

The county contains 472 square miles, or 302,080 acres of land. The number of acres returned for taxation is 291,830, which shows the waste land, village plats, &c., to be but a small fraction over three per cent. The last property valuation, as returned, is as follows:

Real Estate	$4,604,163
Personal Estate	4,101,493
Total for taxation	$8,705.656

But these figures fail entirely to give the *actual* value of the property in the county. It does not include a large amount of property exempt from taxation, and the taxable is only an approximation to the real value.

There are nine villages in the county, viz.: Goshen, Elkhart, Middlebury, Bristol, Millersburg, Waterford, Wakarusha, New Paris and Benton. The first two are important towns; the others are thriving points for local trade.

The St. Joseph river enters the State of Indiana and the county of Elkhart near the northeast corner of Washington township, and runs southwesterly, through Bristol to Elkhart; thence, nearly due west to St. Joseph county. The Elkhart river enters the county near the northeast corner of Benton township, and runs nearly west, through the village of Benton to Jackson township; thence it pursues a northwesterly course through Waterford and Goshen, in Elkhart township, across Jefferson and Concord townships, to Elkhart, where it enters the St. Joseph. It is a fine stream, of considerable volume, and has several valuable mill sites upon it. At Goshen, it is made available for manufacturing purposes to a large extent. The Little Elkhart passes through Middlebury and joins the St. Joseph at Bristol. Christian creek rises in Michigan, enters Elkhart county at the northwest corner of Osolo township, and runs thence nearly south to Elkhart, where it falls into the St. Joseph. Turkey creek enters into the Elkhart river some four miles south of Goshen. Baugo creek and its tributaries serve to water much of the west part of the county.

The Michigan Southern and Northern Indiana Railroad touches the county in York township, runs southwesterly through Bristol and Elkhart to the west line of Baugo township, where it enters St. Joseph county. The air-line branch has its western terminus at Elkhart, and runs almost due southeast, through Goshen and Millersburg, to the northeast corner of Benton township, a distance of about twenty miles, where it leaves the county.

The soil of Elkhart county is invariably of a most excellent quality, and well adapted to the production of fruits, vegetables, and all kinds of grains and grasses. The climate is good, the water excellent and no county in the State of Indiana stands higher in every desirable respect.

Following the course of the St. Joseph, from the old town of Mottville, seven miles, we come to BRISTOL. This town is situated just below where the Little Elkhart enters the St. Joseph, and occupies a beautiful and high plateau of land at a point where the latter river makes a bold but short sweep to the south. The favorable character of the soil, the elevated plateau, the splendid water view from almost every part of the town, the abundance of verdure interspersed with fruits and flowers, and withal that general air of quiet and serenity which everywhere pervades, serve to render Bristol emphatically the

"Loveliest village of the plain."

The surrounding country is very fertile and very beautiful, and the trade of the town, although local, has, from the first settlement of the valley, been important. Quite a large grain trade centers here, and the country round about is noted for the quantity and quality of its orchard fruits.

The Little Elkhart has hitherto furnished sufficient hydraulic power, easily available, for the purposes of the town, and this circumstance has retarded the improvement of the more important St. Joseph. Recently, however, attention has centered upon this latter power, and a substantial company has been formed for the purpose of bringing it into use. From the west end of the town, for over half a mile, the river has such a decided fall as to give the current almost the character of rapids. Here, at a convenient point, the company have purchased a tract of land admirably adapted to the purpose, and are now actively engaged in preparing to build a dam and races. The dam will be very substantial, some three hundred feet long, and giving a head and fall of about eight feet. The main race will be one hundred and fifty feet wide and over one-third of a mile in length. It can be made with very little excavation, by following a depression seemingly intended by nature for the purpose. On either side of this main race are splendid sites for erecting mills, with good facilities for tail races and other conveniences. In a word, there seems to be almost no limit to the facilities and power. Near by are plenty of stone, and on the company's property is now standing abundant timber for all purposes of the improvement. The gentlemen who are engaged in the project are entirely in earnest, and early next year a new field for enterprising manufacturers will be fully opened. The town has now a population of nearly eight hundred, and there is good reason for believing that, before the census of 1870, it will be at least doubled. The Michigan Southern and Northern Indiana Railroad runs through the southern part of the town, and good roads lead in almost every direction.

Probably no person of discernment ever visited the village of ELKHART without being impressed not only with the great beauty of the locality, but with its wonderful adaptation to purposes of business, and especially to manufacturing. The town is situated on a gentle declivity, bounded on the north by the St. Joseph river. The character of the formation, in connection with the dry, hard soil, gives excellent assurance of cleanliness and health. The streets are conveniently laid out, and improved with good taste. Through the easterly part of the town runs the Elkhart river. This is much the lowest portion, but seldom overflowed. In the great freshet of 1855, the Elkhart cut a new channel, east of the old and main one, through which it now discharges a portion of its water into the St. Joseph. This river affords a very desirable water power, which has been successfully, but only partially, improved. A flouring mill, a woolen factory, and some other machinery are located here.

A bridge spans the St. Joseph at the foot of Main street. On the north side is found a large flouring mill and the paper mill of C. Beardsley, Esq. The machinery here is driven by water from Christian creek, a small stream which empties into the St. Joseph about half a mile above. The fall obtained from the Christian is twenty-four feet, and not over half the water is now in use. Here, on a high and commanding table of land, are found some of the finest building spots in the valley or in the West. B. L. Davenport, Esq., is now just completing a splendid mansion here at a cost of over $25,000. It is undoubtedly the best private dwelling in Northern Indiana, and is a specimen of fine taste and good workmanship.

It is almost impossible to say which of the many water powers afforded by the St. Joseph is the best. They are all good, each possessing some advantages peculiar to itself. In this regard Elkhart certainly is not surpassed by any other place, and it is entirely unaccountable how or why the citizens have left it so long unimproved. They seem, however, now to have suddenly opened their eyes to their own best interests, and are evidently in earnest. A short distance above, and nearly adjoining the town, nature has presented them with races nearly ready made to their hands, and with a power sufficient to turn all the machinery at present in the valley. The Elkhart Hydraulic Company are now engaged with a large force in fitting this site for manufacturing purposes. The river is here about one hundred yards wide, and a fine dam is to be thrown across. They are not prepared to say when their works will be completed, and we have no means of knowing what particular inducements they propose to hold out to those seeking business locations. It may be remarked, however, that, in anticipation of the benefits expected to flow from this and other improvements, Elkhart has taken a new start. Numerous buildings, both for business and residences, have recently been erected, and the population is rapidly increasing. In 1860 there were 1433 people here, and this number has probably been just about doubled in the past seven years.

Elkhart is an important railroad point. Here the air and the old line of the Michigan Southern and Northern Indiana road join, it being by the former 133, and by the latter 142 miles to Toledo. The distance to Chicago is 100 miles. The only eating house upon the line is located here. It is kept by Messrs. Patrick & Son, and is in great favor with the public. Its hotel accommodations are complete.

The freight received at and forwarded from Elkhart, for the twelve months ending February 28, 1867, was as follows:

Received,............	8,835,430 lbs;	Revenue,...................	$20,802.41
Forwarded...........	17,662,402 "	"	36,757.60
Total,...........	26,497,832 "		$57,560.01

The number of passengers leaving, for the time above stated, was 26,063, and the earnings from this source were $30,905.30.

There are two newspapers published here, viz.: The *Elkhart Review* and a religious paper called the *Herald of Truth.*

Goshen is the county seat of Elkhart county. It is situated on the east bank of the Elkhart river, and about eighty rods from the lower point of Elkhart Prairie. This prairie is about five miles long by three miles in width, and is noted for the depth and richness of its soil. The site of the town was formerly oak openings. In 1830 the connty seat was located several miles below; but in 1831 it was permanently fixed at Goshen. The land upon which the town stands was entered by the county, and the first lots were sold in the fall of 1831. William Bissell was the first permanent white settler. The first meeting house was built on Sixth street, in the spring of 1833. It belonged to the Methodist Society, and is still in existence, and used as a dwelling house. The first mill was built on Rock Run, about half a mile from the center of the town, by John Carpenter, in 1831. The court house, now standing and in good repair, was commenced in 1832 and completed in the following year. It was the first court house in Indiana north of the Wabash.

In 1860 Goshen had 2,042 inhabitants; at the present time the number does not vary much from 3,200. The town is in a healthy condition, and increasing rapidly in wealth and importance. The Michigan Southern and Northern Indiana Air-line Railroad runs through the western part of Goshen. The freight received and forwarded by this road at and from Goshen, for the year ending February 28, 1867, was as follows:

Received,............	5,688,594 lbs;	Revenue,................	$18,988.74
Forwarded,..........	13,880,520 "	"	29,738.51
Total,...........	19,569,114 "	"	$48,727.25

The number of passengers leaving, for the time stated, was 15,443, from whom was derived a revenue of $18,418.95. Of the freight shipped, one item consisted of about one million feet of black walnut lumber, nearly one-half of which was forwarded by one concern, Hawks Bros. All this and much more ought to have been manufactured at home. The time is near at hand when such a waste of raw material will not be suffered.

The Elkhart river, at Goshen, affords excellent and abundant water power. The Mechanical and Manufacturing Company are now improving this power to its utmost capacity. A substantial dam, two hundred and fifty feet long, one mile above town, will cause nearly the whole of the river to flow through a splendid canal, sixty feet wide at the bottom, and one and a half miles in length. A fall of twenty feet is thus obtained, and many excellent mill sites with plenty of room secured. John W. Erwin, Esq., the engineer of the works, estimates the whole hydraulic power thus made available, to be sufficient for one hundred and fifty runs of stones. In point of durability, security and cheapness, this power is unsurpassed. The gentlemen actively engaged in the work are exhibiting a spirit and liberality which might well be imitated at some other localities. They know that talk will not build a dam, and hence they are investing about $100,000; they know also that in order to draw labor and capital from abroad, they must make known the attractions which they offer; therefore they advertise. Their engagements will all be kept; they have not yet learned the art of repudiation.

Goshen is substantially built, and, especially on the high ground toward its northern limits, presents some very beautiful sites for private residences. The valuation of property for taxable purposes, in 1866, was $715,847. It has two public schools; seven churches; two banks; three hotels; one flouring mill; three agricultural implement factories; one woolen factory; one planing mill and spoke factory; four wagon shops and one tannery. The *Democrat* and the *Times* are the papers published here, both of them respectable in size, handsomely printed and ably conducted.

Middlebury is situated in a township bearing the same name, some five miles nearly south of the railroad. The Little Elkhart runs near by the town, and furnishes power for a flouring mill at no great distance. The situation is delightful. It is in the center of a rich and highly cultivated country, and enjoys quite a large trade. It is rural in its aspect in every particular. A railroad connection, now contemplated, is only required to render it a very desirable place for business or residence. The number of inhabitants is about five hundred.

ST. JOSEPH COUNTY, INDIANA.

The face of St. Joseph County, Indiana, is handsomely diversified, and is in every respect well adapted to all kinds of agricultural industry. The soil may be divided into four kinds, viz.: the light, sandy soil of the original oak openings, or barrens; the black, sandy loam of the thick woods; the deep, vegetable mold of the prairies; and the natural meadows or marshes. The former of these is quick, easily tilled, and is highly prized for the culture of fruit and for horticultural and gardening purposes. It readily responds to the application of fertilizers and to all the appliances of good husbandry. It is no more easily affected by drouth than the prairie or the thick woods; and seldom suffers from excessive rains. The little labor and expense required to bring it from a state of nature under cultivation, secured for it the favorable notice of the early settlers of the county; and many of the first and best farms are located upon it. The densely wooded sections of the county, or as those localities are technically called, the "thick woods," present a soil noted for its strength, certainty and durability. The original growth of the timber upon these lands has been the marvel of all observers; and it has never failed to be a token of the great producing capabilities of the soil when cultivated in the ordinary crops of the farm.

The prairies are Terre Coupee, Greene's, Portage, Harris and Sumption's. Terre Coupee is much the largest, being about nine miles long and an average of three in width. It is quite level and exceedingly fertile. The others are more rolling; but none of them differ essentially from the ordinary prairies of the West, excepting, perhaps, in the high state of cultivation to which careful management has brought them. The marshes are quite numerours, but none of them of much magnitude, except the celebrated Kankakee, which commences two miles from the St. Joseph river, near South Bend. It is but a few years since these lands began to be prized at something near their real value. At present, however, under a proper system of drainage, they have become very desirable. In many localities the coarse marsh grass and useless weeds have given way to fields cultivated in wheat, corn or other crops, or to pasture, or meadow lands thickly set in timothy or blue grass. The *Kankakee* marsh, or perhaps more properly, the Valley of the Kankakee, in particular, presents a remarkable illustration of the benefits of judicious drainage. Here, on four square miles of land, or about two thousand five hundred acres, there has been constructed over twenty miles of ditch, averaging eight feet in width by four feet in depth. These ditches have an average fall of about four feet to the mile. Three-quarters of this drainage is through the outlet of the Kankakee lake into the St. Joseph river, some two miles distant and more than forty feet below the surface of the lake and the surrounding country. Along here is the dividing line between the waters flowing into the St. Lawrence on the one hand and into the Gulf of Mexico on the other. Indeed, so equal is the poise here, that it is frequently impossible to tell in which direction the water is inclined to run when unobstructed or unassisted by art. Some years ago, it is said, the outlet of the Kankakee lake was by the way of the river of that name towards the south-west; and old Government maps make the head of the river in the lake. It is also asserted, upon what seems to be abundant evidence, that by the breaking away of an old beaver dam, the waters of the lake were diverted to the St. Joseph and the lakes.

The Kankakee river is a *very* sluggish, crooked stream, but susceptible of being deepened, widened and straightened at a comparatively small expense. This done, as it doubtless will be, at no distant day, and the system of drainage, now commenced, properly extended, and at least twenty thousand acres of land in this county will be reclaimed and made productive for all purposes of husbandry. Even now, with slight improvements, these natural meadows are capable of being used to great advantage for dairy purposes. The richness of the herbage; the entire exemption from the vicissitudes of drouth; the moderate climate; access to abundant and good water; the low price at which the lands can be purchased and a certainty of a constant increase in their value offer inducements to enterprising dairymen and stock raisers seldom met with elsewhere. If western bound emigrants would give this section an examination they could scarcely fail to choose homesteads and sure fortunes in the midst of an old and desireable country rather than undergo the discomforts, dangers and even want, incident to a settlement in the far off wilds, in the regions of sundown.

A gentleman well acquainted with the dairy business of Herkimer county, New York, and with that portion of the Western Reserve, Ohio, known as *Cheesedom*, among other figures gives us the following estimate of the profits of a dairy farm on these lands:

"One hundred and sixty acres of land will keep fifty cows. The land would cost about $15.00 per acre.

160 acres of land, at $15.00 per acre, is	$2,400
50 cows, at $40.00 each	2,000
Buildings, fencing, etc.,	1,000
Total outlay	$5,400

The net profit for each cow per year has been proved to be not less than $70.00. Then say,

50 cows, first year at $70.00, is	$3,500
50 " second year, at $70.00, is	3,500
Total	$7,000

So that, if a man borrow money to begin with, in two years he could pay it all up and have left as follows:

Cash on hand	$1,600
Cows and improvements	3,000
Land, doubled in value	4,800
Total	$9,400

Which last amount represents the clear profit for two years."

It is easy to double or quadruple this transaction with proportionately increased results. These figures show, at least, that the enterprising dairyman can find an almost unequaled field of labor on the Kankakee. But the value of the Kankakee lands is by no means measured by their adaptation to agricultural uses. It has been demonstrated beyond the shadow of a doubt, that they are overlaid with inexhaustible beds of the best peat in the world! Here is an exemplification of that wonderful principle of compensation which seems to govern in the economy of nature. Immense prairies present to the eye neither tree nor shrub; the forests of the West have been for years undergoing a process of exhaustion; the extraordinary requirements of a new country and the demands of commerce, coupled with an almost inexcusable waste, have already occasioned reasonable fears that the time was approaching, in this section of the country, when even fuel would be an expensive luxury. Within the past ten or twelve years firewood has risen in our market more than two hundred per cent. in value, and even at the present prices, the consumption by our railroads and the rapidly increasing manufactories as well as the requirements for ordinary domestic purposes, have increased these apprehensions. No coal fields are known to be accessible within a reasonable distance. But now all fears are ended. The valley of the Kankakee is ascertained to be a mine of useful wealth and capable of furnishing an inexhaustible supply of fuel at low prices. The following from *Leavitt's Peat Journal* is interesting in this connection:

"There is one peat-bog in Indiana over sixty miles long, with an average width of three miles, extending from South Bend to the Illinois line, along both sides of the Kankakee river. It is possible, at small expense, to lower the bed of this river below the marsh, so as to drain the peat ten or fifteen feet deep. In places it is known to be over forty feet deep. The amount of fuel in this bog is perfectly incalculable, or rather incomprehensible, to any ordinary class of minds. South of the Kankakee, the peat-bogs between there and the Wabash are simply immense, and they are traversed by three railroads.

"The only objection we ever heard to the prairie-marsh peat is that it is generally too light, porous, spongy; too much of it undecomposed fibre of coarse grass and weeds to make good fuel when dried. That objection is all obviated in just such peat when worked in a condensing machine.

Numerous tests have been made with this class of peat from all the extreme Northwestern States, which prove that it is highly combustible, and leaves a very small per cent. of ash. It is the very material needed in all the prairie towns to make gas; for that it is excellent."

It might also have been observed that the northern portion of these peat deposits can be easily drained by cutting a channel into the St. Joseph river at South Bend. Indeed, nearly thirty years ago the late Alexis Coquillard constructed a mill race from the Kankakee river to the St. Joseph, and obtained a sufficient supply of water for two flouring mills and a saw mill, with over forty feet fall. When the dam was thrown across the river at South Bend, these mills were suffered to go into disuse, and finally to decay. For many years they have been out of existence or used for other purposes, and the race is now out of repair and in some places entirely filled up.

Iron ore has been found in some parts of the county in such quantities as to afford hopes of a permanent supply; but it has already been exhausted and the smelting furnaces discontinued.

A good quality of brick clay is sufficiently abundant and conveniently distributed. Both red and yellow brick are made, the latter of a color and quality closely resembling, and not at all inferior to the celebrated Milwaukee brick.

Rich marl deposits are found in many places on the margin and at the bottom of lakes and ponds. The marl is not only valuable as a fertilizer, but is manufactured to some extent into a fair article of lime. It is also said that quite extensive beds of silica of a very fine quality have been discovered. If this be the case, two important ingredients in the composition of glass are ready to the hand of the manufacturer.

The county is well watered by fine springs, clear running streams and several ponds and lakes, and at almost every point the best of water is found by sinking wells from fifteen to twenty-five feet.

The common school system of Indiana is by no means satisfactory to the friends of popular education. It has undergone improvements, from time to time, and a spirit seems to be abroad which will undoubtedly soon ripen into a determination to place the State among the foremost in this regard. In some of the Germanic powers, we are told that education is not only entirely free, but that it is made obligatory upon parents to send their children to school, until a certain age, and that grave disabilities attach to the neglect of the advantages so generously provided. Probably a system of coercion and disabilities is too despotic ever to be adopted under our mild form of government, and that the end sought can be better attained by the stimulas of competitive rewards and popular approbation. However this may be, it is a proposition too plain to admit of serious argument that air and education should be equally pure and free to every minor of sufficient age in the State. No matter of what color, clime, condition or sex, *all* should receive this earnest of the paternal care of a commonwealth, whose honor, power and value can best be preserved and perpetuated by the virtue and intelligence of the ever-rising generation. There are many good common school houses in the county, but as a general thing, the advantages they afford are entirely too intermittent, and in many cases may be said to be almost remittant. The common school should be the best school. It should be the poor man's college and the rich man's pride. Instead of being a convenient place for the occasional restraint of unruly urchins, or an infirmary for pig-headed pedagogues, it should be the fountain of popular intelligence, the index of our civilization and the glory of our State.

The public roads are generally good, but they still offer a wide margin for improvement. There was never but one plank road built within the bounds of the county, except a short one over Grapevine marsh, and that one has differed from other roads only in being much the worst and in the imposition of an exorbitant tax or toll for the privilege of being jolted over an impracticable causeway of decayed and broken plank. Some persons have been guilty of the technical ingratitude of "running" it, and have been subjected to suits at law in consequence; few, however, have been so hopelessly insane as to attempt to *run* upon it. In the summer of 1832, the Great Michigan road, as it was and is still called, was cut through the county. This road reaches from Madison, on the Ohio river, to Michigan City, on lake Michigan, a distance of two hundred and fifty-eight miles. About the same time the Vistula road, running from Toledo (then Vistula) to South Bend, was put in traveling condition. The advent of these two great thoroughfares caused great rejoicing, and subsequently proved highly advantageous in the settlement of the county. They bore about the same relation to the ordinary facilities for locomotion in those days, that the first class railroad of to-day does to them. In May, 1832, the State road from Fort Wayne by the way of Goshen, to South Bend, was surveyed by George Crawford, under the directions of Nathan Coleman, James Blair and Samuel Martin, commissioners. The distance between the termini is seventy-six miles. The distance in this county is ten miles. In the same month a State road, starting at a point where the Michigan road crosses Yellow Creek, by the way of Laporte to the mouth of Trail Creek, was laid out by A. Burnside, commissioner. Fifteen miles of this road were in the then county of St. Joseph. In 1834, the State road through Sumption's prairie to the west line of the State, was located. Mean time various county roads were laid out connecting many already thriving settlements with the county seat.

Ferries were also established across the St. Joseph at South Bend. The first ferry license was granted to N. B. Griffeth, in September, 1831. It was located at the foot of Water street, where the bridge now stands; and Mr. Griffeth was "required to keep a good and sufficient flat or boat, to convey conveniently over said river two horses and a wagon at one time." In January, 1835, another ferry was established at the foot of Market street, and license granted to Alexis Coquillard, who was "required to furnish a boat for said ferry to be at least forty-five feet long by twelve wide." The license fee for a ferry in those days was two dollars per annum. The Circuit Court records for 1833 show that Mr. Coquillard was endeavoring, by a suit at law, to abate the competing efforts of Mr. Griffeth. The records also show the suit to have been a failure.

The act for the formation of St. Joseph and Elkhart counties, approved January 29, 1830, bounds St. Joseph county as follows: "Beginning at range number two west from the second principal meridian of the State of Indiana on the northern line of the State; thence running east to where range number three east intersects the

State line; thence south with the range line thirty miles; thence west to range two west; thence north to the place of beginning."

Thomas J. Evans and Gillis McBane of Cass county, Daniel Worth of Randolph county, John Berry of Madison county, and John Ross of Fayette county, were appointed commissioners to locate the seat of justice.

Section seven provides "that all the territory lying west of said county, to the State line be and the same is hereby attached to the said county of St. Joseph, for civil and criminal jurisdiction; and the citizens residing within the bounds so included, shall be entitled to all the privileges and immunities, and be subject to all the taxes, impositions and assessments of the citizens of St. Joseph."

The bounds of the county have since been somewhat circumscribed, a part going into the composition of Marshall, and a part now belonging to Laporte county. The original south line fell a little below the town of Plymouth.

The county is now bounded north by the State of Michigan, east by Elkhart county, south by Marshall county and west by Laporte county. It was organized the 27th of August, 1830. On that day, in pursuance of the act of the General Assembly, Adam Smith, Lambert McComb and Levi F. Arnold met at the house of Alexis Coquillard and having each presented his commission, as a justice of the peace, from James B. Ray, Governor of the State, took the oath of office before L. M. Taylor, clerk of the county. They then proceeded to elect Lambert McComb president of the board, and St. Joseph county had a legal existence. The first order of the board appointed John D. Lasly county treasurer. Samuel Hanna & Co. and the American Fur Company were each ordered to pay into the county treasury the sum of ten dollars for a license to sell foreign merchandise. Panels of grand and petit jurors were drawn to serve at the term of the circuit court to be held in the following November. It is, however, a matter of doubt whether this court was ever held. Mr. Thomas L. Cotterell, now living at South Bend and who was then sheriff, has an indistinct recollection that it was. He thinks at least one of the county judges was present, that court was duly opened in the woods near the bank of the river, below Water street, and immediately adjourned. Other persons remember to have been present at some time, about that date, when a court was held by county judges; but the first court of which there is any record and at which there was a presiding judge, was held at South Bend, on the 29th day of October, 1832, by Hon. John R. Porter, president judge of the first judicial circuit, to which the county was then attached. It lasted but for one day, and was held in the bar room of Calvin Lilley's hotel, then standing on Michigan street, on the lot now occupied by Messrs. Russ & Ireland. The old building is now in existence and is used by Studebeker Bros. on Jefferson street, as a ware room. Daniel A. Fullerton was sheriff, and Lathrop M. Taylor clerk. Jonathan A. Liston, Elisha Egbert, A. Ingram, Thomas B. Brown, William M. Jenners and C. K. Green were admitted to practice at the bar. The first case recorded in the order book seems to be an illustration of the lines of the poet—

> "'Twas the ominous month of October,
> How the memories rise in my soul!
> How they swell like a sea, in my soul!"

It was Redding *vs.* Redding—petition for a divorce, and was the pioneer case of other thousands which have come after it, bringing an immensity of happiness in their train! An order was made to publish notiec of the pendency of the suit in the *St. Joseph Beacon.* It is pleasant to be able to state that at the next term of the court, Mr. Redding got a bill of divorce from Mrs. Redding, in consideration of which he was ordered to pay the cost of suit in sixty days, or stand the hazard of an attachment. The third case presents Elisha Egbert against Jacob Hardman, in "case for libel." The plaintiff was sent out of court for want of a declaration, and J. A. Liston, attorney for defendant, says: "Received my docket fee." The first criminal case shows Sarah McLelland as respondent, and the lady being interrogated as to how she would acquit herself of the charge of selling spiritous liquors to the Indians, owned up to the "soft impeachment," and paid five dollars for her indiscretion.

The record of the term closes with the following entry:

"The grand jury empanneled to enquire into the body of St. Joseph county, do report, that they have examined the jail of said county, and do find in said jail one prisoner; and farther do find said jail insufficient and uncomfortable. George Holloway, Foreman." Since then the judges for the judicial circuit to which St. Joseph has been attached, have been Gustavus A. Everts, Samuel C. Sample, Ebenezer G. Chamberlain, Thomas S. Stanfield and Andrew G. Osborn, the latter being the present incumbent. Judges Sample and Chamberlain are deceased.

The first conviction for a felony was at a special term of the circuit court, held January 1, 1835, when Alexis Provoncelle was found guilty of burglary, and sent to State prison for three years. This Provoncelle seems to have been a troublesome fellow, for at the November term of the commissioner's court, in 1834, Adam G. Polk was allowed seven dollars for arresting and bringing him from Laporte, and Jennings & Bailey two dollars for "making and repairing handcuffs and fetters for Provoncelle."

The county contains four hundred and sixty-three square miles, or two hundred and ninety-five thousand three hundred and twenty acres of land, about two-thirds of which is under improvement. It is divided into thirteen townships, the population of which in 1860, was as follows:

Township	Population
Portage	4,374
Penn	3,752
German	786
Warren	734
Olive	1,450
Liberty and Lincoln	1,756
Green	960
Center	725
Union	1,461
Harris	349
Clay	914
Madison	1,156
Total for county	18,411

The rate of increase from 1840 to 1860, was for each decade, eighty-four per cent. Taking that as the basis of calculation since 1860, and the population now should be 29,305, and the census of 1870 should show a total of 33,957. These figures are probably very nearly correct.

There are twelve cities and villages in the county, viz: South Bend, Mishawaka, New Carlisle, Plainfield, Terre Coupee,

Weesaw, North Liberty, Walkerton, West Troy, Oceola, Lakeville and Woodland. It is, perhaps, safe to say that some of them are not very large: but the aggregated testimony of citizens from each is to the effect that all are likely to become important towns.

The first steamboat arrived at South Bend in the spring of 1834. She was propelled by a stern wheel, and was called the Matilda Barney. She was hailed with great rejoicings and her advent celebrated with numerous and full-sized libations of red-eye and tangle-leg decoctions.

By an act of the General Assembly of the State, approved January 19th, 1831, the boards of the justices of the peace, in whom the government of counties had previously been vested, were abolished, and the election of three commissioners in each county provided for. An election was accordingly held in the summer of 1831, and Aaron Staunton, David Miller and Joseph Rorer were chosen as commissioners for St. Joseph county. On the 5th of September, the latter two met at the house of Alexis Coquillard, and proceeded to transact county business. Mr. Staunton took his seat the following day.

In May, 1830, the commissioners appointed by the General Assembly met, and located the county seat on the "McCartney Farm," then owned by William Brookfield, about two miles below South Bend. The recorded plot, done in very pretty water colors, announced itself to be "a correct diagram of the county seat called St. Joseph." Each of the Commissioners was honored by having his name given to a street—an honor which, however brilliant in anticipation, has only been realized in successive crops of corn, cabbages and other vegetables, which form the staple productions of the once hopeful county town and embryo city. The town plot of St. Joseph has never been vacated. Its public squares, its corner lots and its magnificent "Broadway," one hundred and twenty-three feet wide, and three-quarters of a mile long, remain to-day very much as the hand of nature left them, illustrating, in their solitude, the moral that

> "The best laid schemes o' mice an' men
> Gang aft agley."

Absolom Holcomb, William M. Hood, Chester Sage and John Jackson, having been appointed by the General Assembly commissioners to re-locate the county seat, met on the 12th day of May, 1831, and were of opinion that the public interest required its removal to South Bend, where they accordingly established it.

February 7th, 1832, Peter Johnson entered into a contract with the county, to build and enclose a court house, for $3,000. The building was accepted by the commissioners in September of the following year. It was not, however, completed until the summer of 1837. In 1854 it was taken down to make way for the present beautiful structure which adorns the city of South Bend.

The first probate court was held at the house of Calvin Lilly, by John Bauker and Chapel W. Brown, associate judges, on the 5th day of January, 1832. The following February James P. Antrim, the first probate judge, appeared and took his seat.

The duplicate for 1840 shows the tax levy to be $3,038.89. The population that year was 6,425. In 1866 the levy was $92,136.25, and the population about 28,000. In the latter year the valuation of property for taxable purposes was

Real Estate,	$4,923,305
Personal Property,	2,750,300
Total,	$7,673,605

The true valuation of the property of the county would, however, show an amount more than double the above; probably not less than $18,000,000. It will, therefore, be seen that the taxes are but little more than nominal.

In the winter of 1845 a community, suggested, probably, by the system of economics elaborated by the French philosopher, Charles Fourier, was established on the "McCartney Farm," before mentioned, and about two miles below South Bend. It was a joint stock company, incorporated by the name of the "Philadelphia Industrial Association." Its objects were economical and social. Its operations continued about two years. Hon. Wm. C. Talcott, of Valparaiso, Indiana, favors us with the following reminiscences in relation to it:

"I think old Mr. McCartney was the first president, and I was secretary, during almost its entire existence. It was chiefly through my influence that the association was formed and managed. There were, probably, more than a hundred persons, old and young, connected with us, from first to last; but I should not think more than about seventy living on the premises at once. During a part of the time they ate at a common table. * * * The main cause of their dissolution, I have ever believed, was that Mr. McCartney violated his promise to invest his whole tract of land; and after we were fully organized and on the ground ready to receive the title and use the land, he withheld all of the valuable and available portion, and turned us off with the broken, marshy land, lying between the road and the river, at twenty dollars per acre, the appraised price of the entire tract."

The cause of the failure, "in a nut shell," was probably this: McCartney, with his natural shrewdness, if that is the proper term, encouraged and co-operated with the association for the purpose of getting his land cleared up and improved for nothing. He succeeded, but the association did not.

The early history of St. Joseph county was, according to the relation of the old settlers who now survive, checkered by those vicissitudes common to the settlement of all new countries. There was little capital and less conveniences. Roads were few and far between. Schools, churches and other appliances and promoters of civilization were rare, yet highly prized and eagerly sought. Fevers of untold types and multifarious phases swelled the aggregate of miseries and brought many a robust settler to an early grave. Indians and doctors were almost equally abundant; and even lawyers, not in pairs, but in packs, came poking their angular faces into the most promising settlements of this incipient Eden. Speculators swarmed in land offices, made paper towns, "played out," and left wiser and poorer if not better than they came. To illustrate something of this we give a brief outline of the adventures and misadventures of one or two of the early settlers of this county. The pictures, with slight variation, will find a counterpart in every section of the country.

Abraham R. Harper left his old home in Myerstown, Lebanon county, Pennsylvania, October 1, 1835, to seek a location in the new country. He took the stage for Pittsburgh, and from there, on the new steamer Pocahontas, went to Natchez. Bound for Natchetoches, he remained at the mouth of Red river, waiting for a boat, six days. The hotel he staid at was fifteen by twenty feet, and set on blocks six feet high to keep it out of the water. About fifteen Indians were in the attic and some five hundred negroes outside, all waiting to go up the river. Here, for the first time he saw the beauties of the "peculiar institution," and took his first degree in anti-slavery doctrine. He landed at Natchetoches Sunday afternoon, and saw about five hundred gamblers hard at work at their usual vocation. There he staid a week, in which time two men were murdered and many more robbed. He then went, *via* New Orleans, to St. Louis, thence to Pittsburgh, and again over the mountains by stage, arriving at home about the middle of January, 1836. He started a second time, about the first of April, in company with some fifteen other voyagers, by stage to Pittsburgh. Thence, by steamer, the party went to St. Louis. All took deck passage, and some being short of money helped wood to pay part of their expenses. From St. Louis they came by steamer to Beardstown, and thence walked to Peoria, from which latter place Mr. Harper came, *via* Chicago, by stage to South Bend, where he arrived about the first of May. Here he decided to settle, and immediately ordered $10,000 worth of goods from Philadelphia. The goods were shipped on board the barge Detroit from Buffalo, the first of June, and this was the last he heard from them until the last of September. Going in pursuit of his goods, Mr. Harper stopped a few days at Michigan City, and then walked to Chicago, on the beach of the lake. Just as he arrived at Chicago his goods came in, and in six days he got them shipped on the schooner Sea Serpent and sailed for Michigan City. Before he had been out two hours a terrible storm came on, and the vessel made for St. Joseph, where it finally arrived in safety. In two days thereafter they made sail again for Michigan City, where they soon arrived, the weather being fine; but in half an hour after landing, another storm commenced, and drove all the vessels in that port ashore. In the morning he found the vessel containing his goods beached and all the crew gone. He took charge of the craft himself, and got out all his dry goods. That night another storm drove the vessel into the mouth of Trail creek, and all the groceries were lost. He had the damages assessed, and commenced drying the goods on the sand hills. By the time that labor was completed, another shipment of about the value of $10,000 arrived, and he sent the whole, by teams, to

South Bend, where he commenced business about the first of November, 1836, five months after his first shipment from Buffalo.

On the morning of July 4th, 1836, while waiting for his goods, Mr. H. started on foot for Lafayette. By three o'clock he was at Judge Polk's house on the Tippecanoe river. Next morning he took breakfast at Logansport, and beat the stage into Lafayette. He was on a business tour, taking orders for goods, and this is a specimen of "drumming" in those days. Some things have changed since then.

The reign of wild cat money was in 1836–7. The "sickly season" was 1838. The crops failed in 1839, and in 1840 was the great panic, at which time Harper, Smith & Co. had over $40,000 standing out, which was probably more than twice as much as all the money in the county. Mr. H. moved back to Pennsylvania some twelve years ago.

John H. Harper left Hanover, Lebanon county, Pa., on the first day of May, 1837, and, traveling with his own conveyance, arrived at South Bend in twenty-three days. The journey can now be made in twenty-four hours. He was one of the fourth generation of the same name who had lived on the same place, known as "Harper's Place," for one hundred and forty years. He was one of the firm of Harper, Smith & Co., and was intimately connected with many of the early improvements of the county. He has been much in public life, and still resides at South Bend, an honored citizen and a genial gentleman.

Such was life in those days, and such are some of the incidents of the past generation, in St. Joseph county. We have undertaken to present only gleanings—"here a little, and there a little"—a mere skeleton of what ought to be written. Some may gain a few moment's satisfaction from the perusal—others may skip it if they please.

MISHAWAKA.—In July, 1833, A. M. Hurd laid out and platted the village of "St. Joseph Iron Works," about four miles above South Bend, on the south bank of the St. Joseph river. On the first day of January, 1835, an election was held, and the following village trustees were elected, viz.: James White, John J. Deming, Samuel Stancliff, Henry DeCamp and Alexander Sanderlands. This was the first village organization in the county.

In June, 1836, Joseph Bartell, James R. Lawrence and Grove Lawrence laid out the town of "Indiana City," situated on the north side of the river, opposite St. Joseph Iron Works. The plat of this town shows a race of extraordinary length, but, like a line in mathematics, it had length without breadth or thickness—it was never excavated. At what time or under what circumstances these two towns became incorporated under the present name of Mishawaka, is a matter upon which "commentators do not agree." The fact is, however, undisputed that all the territory embraced in them, and much more, is now comprised within the beautiful town of Mishawaka. Mr. Merrifield, in his excellent reminiscences, published several years ago, says that "Mr. Terrington, the intelligent clerk of Mr. Hurd, had sufficient taste to appreciate the superior beauty and adaptation of the Indian name; and when, the next year, an effort was made to get a post office established here, it was at his suggestion that it was called Mishawaka. By an amendment of the act of incorporation, this afterwards became the legal name of the town." This may account for the change of name of St. Joseph Iron Works, but how came Indiana City combined with it?

The Indian word Mishawaka is said to signify "swift water;" but by some it is said to mean "thick-woods rapids." Either interpretation would be descriptive of the location.

The town is situated on both banks of the St. Joseph, within about a mile of the most southern point of that river. The site is one of very great natural beauty, and art and taste have added largely to its original loveliness. On the south side there is a gentle upward slope from the river bank, far off beyond the limits of the town. Here, embowered beneath a profusion of natural and cultivated trees, shrubbery and flowers, is built the main portion of Mishawaka. On the opposite side the banks are more precipitous, forming a high table of land, seemingly designed by nature for its present uses.

In 1833, A. M. Hurd commenced building a blast furnace, which was completed and put in successful operation the following year. The population at the end of 1833 was about one hundred. There was no ferry, but there was an excellent ford near where the dam is now located.

On the 22d day of January, 1835 the "St. Joseph Iron Company was incorporated, and immediately began building a dam across the river, which was completed in the summer of 1836. This was the first dam ever built across the St. Joseph, and it stands to-day as solid and firm as at the moment of its completion, a monument to the sagacity and ability of its builders. A. M. Hurd, John J. Deming and John H. Orr were the corporators and active men in this company. Judge Deming was born in Vermont, had been a school teacher, possessed a good, cultivated and refined intellect, and contributed largely to the social advancement of the town. He died several years ago in California. Mr. Orr was an Englishman, educated and capable, and just such a man as any place ought to be proud of. He now lives in Cleveland, Ohio. Mr. Hurd was originally from New York, lived some time at Detroit, and was an excellent business man and a good citizen. He still survives. The St. Joseph Iron Company continued to operate their blast furnaces until 1856, when the supply of ore failed. They also established a foundry, and put in operation other machinery, which has been of incalculable benefit to the place. They still own a large share of the hydraulic power, and are also engaged in trading and manufacturing on a very liberal scale. It is now controlled by John Niles, Esq., his son Henry G. Niles, Oliver T. Niles, and Allan Sisson.

The hydraulic power at this place is unsurpassed at any point on the river, and the facilities for erecting mills are most excellent. The town is situated upon the Michigan Southern and Northern Indiana Railroad, and is easily accessible from east or west. The Peninsular road, from Port Huron to Chicago, will soon pass through the town. The surrounding country is one of extraordinary fertility, and the healthfulness of the place is undisputed. The St. Joseph Iron Company have still a large amount of power to dispose of at reasonable rates and on easy terms.

In early times there was great rivalry between Mishawaka and South Bend. They were less than four miles apart, and the advantages which they offered differed very slightly, except that the latter had the honor of being the county seat. The bitterness of those days has, however, subsided, and it is now seen that the interests of the two places are identical. Before many years the thriving borders of the two towns will meet, and it is not at all improbable that, in the course of time, they will be joined in one municipality. Already a street railroad is contemplated between the two places.

Not only was the first dam across the St. Joseph built at Mishawaka, but, if we except the territorial ones at Mottville and Bertrand, the first bridge, also. As early as 1837 the enterprising citizens, by subscription, erected a substantial structure across the river, which has since given way to the present one. Many years ago the steamboat Diamond was wrecked by running against a pier of this bridge, and one life was lost. Perhaps the cylinder of the engine of this boat was the one made classic by Hon. H. H. Riley, in his Puddleford Papers. At the close of 1837 the population had reached about one thousand.

In 1839 the first flouring mill was erected, with two runs of stones. In 1842 there were six runs of stones in operation, with a daily capacity of two hundred barrels of flour. Now there are three mills with fourteen runs of stone, and a daily capacity of over five hundred barrels of flour. They are as follows:

Mishawaka Mills,......	A. B. Judson & Co.....	5	runs of	stones.
Ripple Mills,..........	A. Cass & Co	5	"	"
St. Joseph Mills,.......	Kuhn & Brother.......	4	"	".

The quality of flour made at these mills is most excellent, standing at all times at the very top of the market. In 1865, 30,436 barrels of flour were shipped east by railroad from Mishawaka. A very large quantity also went west.

The freight received and forwarded at and from Mishawaka, for the year ending February 28, 1867, by railroad, was as follows:

Received,............	7,318,502 lbs;	Revenue, ...	$15,675.57
Forwarded,..........	10,518,459 "	"	23,587.22
No. passengers leaving	6,944	"	8,159.45
Total earnings for the year			$47,422.24

The excess of outgoing over incoming freight is a circumstance which indicates a healthy industrial condition.

The river at Mishawaka is about one hundred yards wide, and the fall over the dam is eight feet. The natural fall at these rapids, in a distance of but a few rods, has been ascertained by actual measurement to be two feet and nine inches. The race on the south side is about four hundred yards in length; and the one on the north side over two hundred yards. On either side there is opportunity for an almost indefinite extension and there is at all times, an abundance of water for all conceivable purposes. Indeed, but a very small portion of this valuable power has, as yet, been appropriated. The manufactories are, however, gradually and successfully increasing. There are now in operation three flouring mills, two saw mills, four wagon factories, four furniture factories, one agricultural implement factory, two ax and edge tool factories, one woolen factory, five barrel factories, one basket factory, and one sash, blind and door factory. The mammoth wagon factory of Messrs. Geo. Milburn & Co., is worthy of particular notice. The products of this establishment are sold all the way from lake Erie to the Rio Grande. It gives employment to about one hundred hands, and the value of wagons, carriages, etc., turned out is nearly $150,000 per annum. Judson, Montgomery & Co. have here the largest furniture factory in the State of Indiana. The main building is forty by one hundred and eighty feet and three stories high. They have besides three large warehouses. At present they give employment to seventy hands, and will soon increase the number to over one hundred. They use over a million and a half feet of lumber in a year and have constantly on hand and seasoning about two million feet. Last year they made over sixteen thousand bedsteads, and this is only one item. Messrs. Martin, and Bless, Kena & Co. have large furniture establishments and are doing a thriving and increasing business. The St. Joseph Iron Company has long stood among the foremost manufactories of the West in the line of agricultural implements. Its annual products amount in value to about $150,000.

The value of manufactured products for the past year, is estimated as follows:

Flouring Mills, shipped and custom work	$500,000
Wagons and Carriages	200,000
Furniture	240,000
Saw Mills	25,000
Sash, Doors and Blinds	25,000
Agricultural Implements	150,000
Axes and Edge Tools	30,000
Barrels	20,000
Miscellaneous	120,000
Total	$1,310,000

The population of the town was in 1860, according to the census returns, 1,486. Careful and competent judges estimate it at the present time at 3,000 at least.

There has been more interest taken in public schools here than in any other part of the county, and with good success. The first school house was built in 1834, and Miss Sheldon of White Pigeon, was the first teacher. There is now, however, great need of an educational institution of a high order, a need which can, perhaps, be best supplied by improved, if not perfected public schools. The enterprising and progressive people of Mishawaka are not the ones to suffer long a want which can be supplied, and it may be safely predicted that all requisite intellectual advantages will soon be afforded.

In 1841, Wilbur F. Storey issued the *Mishawaka Tocsin*, the the first newspaper published here. It was edited and published by himself. Mr. Storey has since made his mark in the world as a journalist. He was for several years at the head of the *Detroit Free Press*, and has been for a long time, and now is, the able conductor of the *Chicago Times*. At the end of the first year the *Tocsin* was purchased by George Merrifield, who continued it until 1845, when it was sold to Thomas Jernigan, and removed to South Bend.

In 1846, S. P. Hart started the *Mishawaka Bee*, which, after being published about two years, was discontinued.

The *Free Press* was issued by D. C. Ireland, in 1853, and continued by him for two years, when he sold out to L. A. Elliot. Mr. Ireland now resides in Oregon City, and is editor of a paper there. Mr. Elliot is dead. Mr. Elliot changed the name to *Mishawaka Enterprise*, and, after publishing it for nearly two years, sold it to Mr. Archibald Beal, who is at present one of the editors of the *St. Joseph Valley Register* at South Bend. In 1865, the *Enterprise* passed into the hands of N. V. Brower, by whom it is now successfully and ably conducted.

There was, several years ago, published by P. T. Russell, for a short time a religious paper called the *Investigator*. It advocated the peculiar views of the Christian denomination.

South Bend.—The city of South Bend is situated on both banks of the river, in Portage township, near a point where the

St. Joseph suddenly turns from a nearly west course and stretches away with a rapid current, northward, into the State of Michigan. The site of the city is extremely picturesque and beautiful. On the west bank of the river an abrupt bluff rises to the height of some forty feet, thence, for a distance varying from one-fourth to three-quarters of a mile, extends a beautiful table of gravelly land, eminently fitted for purposes of building. Then ensues another elevation, of some ten or twelve feet, with a succession of fine, dry and eligible building ground. This is the old town of South Bend. The location is elevated and commanding, and the character of the soil and the excellent facilities for perfect drainage, are a perpetual guarantee of healthy and attractive places of residence, and dry, hard and durable thoroughfares for locomotion. The rich, sandy loam, of which the soil is composed, forms abundant nutriment for the healthy and rapid growth of innumerable shade and ornamental trees, indigenous to the locality, among which may be mentioned the sugar and silver maple, the elm, the sycamore, the walnut, and the oak; while gardens are filled with thrifty apple, pear, peach, plum, cherry and quince trees, and an abundance of the smaller fruits. The streets are wide and regular, crossing each other at right angles, and at convenient intervals. The grades are uniform, with a sufficient fall toward the river to secure perfect drainage and afford a never-failing auxiliary to the natural healthfulness of the place. The business houses are capacious and convenient, while many of them, by their imposing appearance, impart a metropolitan air to the city. The private residences, many of which are of brick, are generally neat and tasteful, and frequently illustrate some of the most modern and artistic achievements in architecture.

On the east side a wide and rich bottom stretches away from the margin of the river, with a gentle aclivity, until it is lost in the romantic hillsides bordering upon the domain of Notre Dame du Lac. This, until recently, was the village of Lowell. It is now a part of the city. Through the bottom, and sufficiently elevated to be secure from inundations, runs a capacious race, affording a large number of excellent mill sites and abundant hydraulic power. Here are also many fine business localities and desirable lots for private dwellings. The time cannot be far distant when this now sparsely settled delta will be the industrial center, not only of the city, but of Northern Indiana.

Nature has here been lavish of those advantages which only require the developing hand of human enterprise to yield rich and sure returns. Here the whole machinery of Lowell or Lawrence might be driven without intermission, and still there would be power left for new comers and new enterprises—not among the rugged hills and rocky mountains of New England, where the chief "agricultural productions" are school houses and men, but in the very lap of luxuriance and plenty, and at the doorway of the capacious market of the great West.

But, from the very general description thus given, the man of business can gather very little which will be practically important to him. For all purposes of an ordinary county seat or post town it might suffice; but South Bend claims to be something more—to be at least the vigorous and promising beginning of a large and important manufacturing and business city—not only the trading center of a rich and fast developing county, but a point of unusual facilities in the direct channel of a never-ceasing stream of immigration. We, therefore, leave "glittering generalities" and proceed to the consideration of particulars.

The first white settlement at South Bend was made by Alexis Coquillard, in the spring of 1824. This was also the first in the county. Mr. Coquillard was an Indian trader and agent for the North American Fur Company, then actively managed by John Jacob Astor. He was a Frenchman, born in Montreal, which place he left at an early age, and spent most of his active life among the Indians. He was a man of powerful frame, active temperament and genial disposition. As a business man he was enterprising, energetic and generally successful. His relation of the early events in this country was graphic and exceedingly interesting. He was a great favorite with the Indians, who once elected him a chief, and over whom he had an extraordinary influence. He was accidentally killed by a fall, in January, 1855, at the age of about sixty.

Lathrop M. Taylor settled here in September, 1827. He was also an Indian trader, and agent for the firm of Samuel Hanna & Co., of Fort Wayne. He was the first clerk of the county, has, for forty years, mixed actively in all the events that make an interesting history, and still survives, hale and hearty, to relate his varied experiences. In the same year several settlers came in who are yet living, among whom was Samuel L. Cotterell, the first sheriff.

The town was laid out and platted the 28th of March, 1831, by Coquillard and Taylor. The first charter election was held October 3d, 1835, at which time William P. Howe, Horatio Chapin, Peter Johnson, John Massey and James A. Mann were elected trustees. The village organization was abandoned in 1837, but in 1845, when the small pox was so prevalent that unusual sanitary precautions and police regulations became imperative, it was revived. In May, 1865, an organization under a city charter was effected, by the election of William G. George, Esq., as Mayor, and Wm. Miller, John Klingle, first ward; Thos. S. Stanfield, Hon. William Miller, second ward; Israel Sweet and John Gallagher, third ward, councilmen. Since then the village of Lowell has been incorporated with the city, and forms the fourth ward.

The population of South Bend, including the late village of Lowell, was, in 1840, according to the census of that year, 728; in 1850, it was 1,653; and in 1860 it had reached 3,832. A recent publication recklessly and foolishly puts the present number at 9,750, which is about 2,000 too much. A liberal and fair estimate results in about 7,750, which is probably within bounds and not far from exact. At the present rate of increase, and with the unusual inducements for men of capital, business or leisure to settle here, it is quite safe to say that the census of 1870 will show a population of over 10,000.

In 1842 the South Bend Manufacturing Company was chartered, and in the following year the company built a substantial dam across the St. Joseph river, which affords an abundant and almost exhaustless hydraulic power, and which has contributed largely toward the permanent prosperity of the place.

The first determined effort at utilizing the great water power afforded by the St. Joseph, at South Bend, was made by Joseph Fellows, Garrett V. Dennison, Thomas W. Alcott, James McKown, William J. Worth, and John Van Buren, all of the State of New York. Most of these men will be recognized as having figured largely in public life; Judge McKown, General

Worth and John Van Buren, especially, have since been widely known. They purchased the land in 1835. In 1837 they laid out a town opposite South Bend, which was called Dennison. It was afterwards called Lowell, and now forms part of the city of South Bend, as before observed. They commenced digging a race, and had a large amount of timber in readiness for building head gates, locks, &c., when the scheme suddenly collapsed, and the project was abandoned. Alexis Coquillard afterwards came into possession of the premises, and he made large improvements on the race. It is now owned by the South Bend Hydraulic Company, a corporation with a capital of $100,000, composed of *live* men who are now engaged in enlarging the capacity of the power and perfecting it for an almost unlimited use. This company has a right to the use of one-half the water flowing in the river, which is equivalent, at a very moderate estimate, to a sixty-horse power for one hundred water wheels. They have a race five hundred yards in length, and it is now in process of improvement. When completed it will be one thousand yards long, one hundred feet wide, and seven feet deep. The fall of the river, over the dam, is eight feet on the west side and nine feet on the east side. The fall from the head to the mouth of the race is twenty-eight inches. Such a hydraulic power in New England would ensure the building of a city of fifty thousand inhabitants in two years. It would set the capitalists of Boston half crazy in an hour; and agitate the "hub of creation" to the extremity of every spoke. But when it is considered that here this power is, in reality and for every practical purpose, worth one hundred per cent. more than it would be if located in any part of New England, who can compute its value? But when we go further and state the fact, which exists to-day, that this is but one-half of the power now in perpetual motion at South Bend, and the additional one that for a distance of more than one hundred and fifty miles, the St. Joseph is competent to duplicate the whole of it every five miles, the senses are astounded, and every attempt at computation becomes not only futile but farcical. It requires no effort of the imagination, but only the exercise of those more sober and reflective faculties which enter into the mental composition of the successful business man, to see that the time is approaching—that it is now almost here—when this valley must and will be an industrial bee hive, unsurpassed on the continent of America. The South Bend Hydraulic Company are now prepared to lease or sell, on the most favorable terms, a large portion of this power to persons desirous of availing themselves of its great advantages. On another page of this work will be found their views and proposals in detail.

One-half of this immense power is owned by the South Bend Manufacturing Company, alluded to above. Their race extends over one thousand feet, on the west side of the river, and every water lot upon it, but two or three, is already occupied. Right there, under the hill, in those unpretending mills and factories, lie the main-springs of the prosperity of this infant city. Wars may come, the elements may be unpropitious, crops may fail—no matter! The prosperity of the city is not retarded. The hum of industry goes on. Labor reaps its full reward; capital is safely employed and richly remunerated, and wealth, with all its comforts and blessings, pours in, in an uninterrupted stream.

An idea of the general business of the city may be gathered, to some extent, by inspecting the advertisements contained in this book. It may be noticed, however, that all the business firms are not represented. There are three classes which do not advertise: 1st, the oldest settlers, who are generally well known and already rich; 2d, those so poor that they cannot pay for an advertisement; 3d, those who have too little enterprise and who are, withal, too mean to pay for a little publicity.

Something of the magnitude of the manufacturing interests here is represented in the facts and figures following: There are in operation three flouring mills; four wagon and carriage factories; three furniture factories; three saw mills; two sash, blind and door factories; one pump factory; one chair factory; two tanneries; one mattress factory; one woolen factory; six barrel factories; one clover thresher factory; one seed drill factory, and one agricultural implement factory.

The following table shows the value of the products of these different branches of industry for the year 1866:

Flouring Mills (shipping and custom work)	$600,000
Wagons and Carriages,...........................	310,000
Furniture, ...	220,000
Saw Mills,...	25,000
Sashes, blinds and doors, ...	55,000
Agricultural Implements,..........................	205,000
Hubs, spokes and felloes,.........................	45,000
Pumps, ...	10,000
Chairs, ...	35,000
Tanneries, ...	50,000
Mattress and Woolen goods,........................	55,000
Barrels, ...	25,000
Clover Threshers,.................................	75,000
Clothing, Boots and Shoes, &c.,...................	200,000
	$1,910,000

All branches of manufacture are in a healthy condition. The demand for all articles produced more than equals the supply. Sales are easily made, and with little outlay for commissions. Wages are liberal and promptly paid. Living is cheap, and operatives, as well as employers, are thriving and independent.

The report of the Michigan Southern and Northern Indiana Railroad Company, for the year ending February 28th, 1867, gives the amount of freight received and forwarded at this point, with the revenue derived therefrom, as follows:

Freight received,.....	13,320,269 lbs;	Revenue, ...	$29,769.53
Freight forwarded,....	13,346,972 "	"	28,635.64
Total,..........	26,667,241 "		$58,405.17

The singular uniformity in the amount of incoming and outgoing freight, and the revenue derived therefrom, will be noticed.

The revenue derived from passengers leaving South Bend, by this road, for the year, is $34,100.57, being exceeded in amount by only each of four stations on the whole line, viz.: Chicago, Toledo, Detroit and Adrian, all termini of roads.

It may not already have escaped the notice of the intelligent reader that if, in the course of time, the whole hydraulic power of the St. Joseph at South Bend should be exhausted, in driving the machinery which enterprise, capital and labor will set in motion, a very large additional power is easily available from the

Kankakee river. A comparatively small outlay of means would bring from that source a current of water which, with the great fall of between forty and fifty feet, would move a large amount of machinery. The feasibility of such an enterprise was tested and proved by Mr. Coquillard, at an early day, as elsewhere stated.

The time is approaching when the city will require a supply of pure water over and beyond that now obtained from wells. The Kankakee lake is at hand, with its abundant stores, which, at a moderate expense, can be made to flow into every household; or, if thought preferable, water can be forced from the St. Joseph to an elevated distributing reservoir. The city, with commendable forecast, has already secured water power sufficient for such an emergency, which will be used at an early day.

South Bend was a railroad station long before the Northern Indiana road was seriously thought of. The road which ran through it was called, in a metaphorical way, "the underground railroad;" not because it was a sort of miraculous tunnel beneath the soil, but on account of the fact that although the trains were known to be frequent, very few persons ever saw them. The enterprising managers were singularly nocturnal in their habits, and a large proportion of the passengers appeared to have been born under the rule of the "ebon throne." It was liberally patronized, but the dividends to stockholders were "few and far between." It is said, however, that a large amount is placed to their credit in a divinely chartered savings bank, where moth doth not corrupt, and where thieves do not break through and steal. Its operations were carried on, it must be confessed, in opposition to law—that is to say, the fugitive slave law; and, if slavery should turn out, after all, to have been a divine institution, as many contend it will, then it must be conceded that it defied "God, man and the devil." At any rate, its business was large, if not profitable; and, although the dividends were small, the assessments were sometimes frightfully large. One fine morning the booming of cannon was heard in Charleston harbor in South Carolina; and at the same moment this railroad vanished, like the gossamer web of the fairies at the crowing of the cock. As Byron died, according to the pious Pollock, because there was no more to drink, so this extraordinary institution became defunct on account of the sudden falling off of that peculiar traffic which gave it vitality. South Bend has, however, had her experiences in the business; whether they were sweet or bitter is a question which may be safely left to the determination of individual tastes. As a matter of history, something of these experiences should be here chronicled.

John Norris, of Boone county, Kentucky, claimed to be the owner of David Powell, his wife and four children, all of African descent, but not then exactly our fellow-citizens. These persons had been passengers on the "underground railroad," and had located in Cass county, Michigan. After searching Southern Indiana for about two months, Norris, in the middle of a September night, in 1849, with a party of eight men, forcibly broke into Powell's house, and, drawing pistols and knives, compelled the wife and three children to follow him. Hurrying them off, bound with cords, they placed them in covered wagons and started for Kentucky. Alarm was soon given and pursuit commenced. They were overtaken at South Bend, about thirty miles from where they started. A writ of *habeas corpus* was sued out, and the parties were discharged by Hon. Elisha Egbert, probate judge. "Norris, in the meantime, had gathered his men around the captives, and the moment the decision was announced they seized the captives with one hand, brandished their weapons with the other, threatening to shoot the first man that interfered. This was while the judge was on the bench, and before any adjournment had been announced. Everything had been perfectly quiet up to this moment, but upon this display of force, the people rose to their feet highly excited. * * * Mr. Liston, one of the counsel, jumped upon a table, and called upon the Kentuckians to shoot all who interfered, and they would be justified in so doing. His language was most violent and abusive toward the citizens, and did much to fan the excitement." Suffice it to say that the captives were never returned to slavery; but a law suit was commenced between Norris and Leander B. Newton, George W. Horton, Edwin B. Crocker, Solomon W. Palmer, David Jodon, William Wilmington, Lot Day, Jr., and Amable M. Lapiere, citizens of South Bend, to recover the value of the negroes and other damages. It was vigorously fought, but Norris beat, and some of the defendants were rendered homeless and penniless by the sale of their property. Mr. Norris has probably had other experiences in the slave line since then, quite as exciting, but perhaps less profitable. He and his ruffianly attendants succeeded in making South Bend classic ground, and in arousing in Northern Indiana a spirit which he, or some of his, may possibly have since met in the "sunny South" amid the gleam of bayonets and other things of that sort.

There are several public buildings in the city worthy of particular remark. The court house is a fine structure of cut Athens stone, with a front ornamented with seven Corinthian columns. It was built in 1854, at an expense of $35,000. The jail was erected in 1860. It is a model building for the purpose it is intended to subserve; indeed, exteriorly it is the handsomest building in the county. It cost about $35,000. The new post office, built in 1865, is a tasteful and well arranged structure. There are five public school houses, four of which are of brick, and are intended for ward schools. A large and elegant Union school house is contemplated and will soon be built. Neither city nor county owes any debt occasioned by the construction of these buildings.

The first church in the city, and in the county also, was erected by the Methodist, in 1832, on Michigan street, between Lafayette and Jefferson streets. Samuel Good and Adanijah Rambo were the builders. It was never used as a church, the workmanship and materials being so poor that the trustees refused to receive it. Thus an effort to cheat the Lord was defeated and two enterprising gentlemen disgusted. It is still in existence and is occupied as a barn, near the south-east corner of Michigan and Wayne streets. In 1835 the Methodists were successful in building a church on the west side of Main street, north of Market street, which was occupied for many years. There are now nine churches, including the chapel on the east side. They are, the Presbyterian, Methodist, Baptist, Dutch Reformed, two Catholic, German Lutheran, Universalist, United Brethren and Christian Disciples. The Church of the Sacred Heart, of Notre Dame, although outside the city limits, is easy of access and largely attended by persons living in South Bend. This church has a chime of twenty-four bells, cast in France, and ranging in tone two octaves, from G to G. The largest bell was spoiled by a crack, some years ago, and another has been recently received from

France to replace it. This bell weighs over fourteen thousand pounds. There is only one larger bell in the United States, and but two upon the continent. It is claimed that this bell, when in place, can be heard for a distance of twenty miles.

The first bank at South Bend was established in 1838. It was a branch of the Indiana State Bank, and had a capital of $102,000. When the charter expired, in 1856, and the Bank of the State of Indiana was incorporated, a branch was organized here with a capital of $100,000, afterwards increased to $150,000, which continued until the First National Bank, with a capital of the latter amount, took its place. In addition, there is now in operation the St. Joseph County Bank, which is not a corporation. Under the late free banking law of the State, the Bank of South Bend was located here by some eastern capitalists. It was little more than a redemption office, but was one of the few of its class that never suspended.

The property of the city is valued for taxation at $2,522,977. This is less than one-half its actual value, which may be safely put at $6,000,000. The levy for 1867 is only about sixty cents on the hundred dollars, a fact hardly to be credited by the over taxed citizens of New York, Chicago, and other large cities. Perhaps when South Bend is rejoicing in her hundred thousand inhabitants, some victim of municipal rapacity in that "good time coming," may point back to this item as evidence of the unsophisticated innocence of primitive councilmen.

It is difficult to particularise the business interests of South Bend; yet it is proper to do so to some extent. The Messrs. Studebaker Bro's have established a business in the last dozen years which is really an "institution" of the city. Their carriages, buggies, wagons, sleighs, and all other articles in their line, are known throughout the West and Southwest. From a small beginning, these persistent workers have reached an enviable position. More than one hundred and thirty men are constantly employed by them, and they annually produce nearly a quarter of a million dollars worth of manufactured articles. A. Coquillard & Co. are engaged in the same branch of industry, and on a very large scale. Jacob Strayer & Co. are turning out large numbers of their celebrated seed drills. It is said that any farmer who has thirty acres of wheat to sow can pay for the drill by the increase in the crop for one year by using one of them. Liphart & Co. take the lead in furniture; and Lantz Bros. & Co. have no successful competitors in the manufacture and sale of clothing. The superior quality of the flour made by the mills here is well known to the trade and to consumers. In fact, the large manufacturing interest of South Bend is in a healthy condition and is conducted by earnest, competent and every way reliable men. Nothing is overdone and there is plenty of room for additional industry and capital. A paper mill, a cotton and woolen factory, all on a large scale, are much needed and would receive co-operation and assistance from the foremost citizens of the place. Indeed, almost any branch of business that requires a good water power, cheap living and a constant market, would thrive here. To all other inducements South Bend adds a quiet, moral, healthy and in all respects desireable place of residence. Property is low compared with other places of equal facilities, and a generous welcome awaits all new comers.

No other city in the State presents so varied and excellent facilities for the training and education of youth, of both sexes, as South Bend; and probably these facilities are not excelled in any part of the continent. As early as 1832, when the chief part of the inhabitants of the valley were the red men of the forest—the Miamis and the Pottawatomies—the Rev. Stephen T. Badin visited the spot now known as Notre Dame, and, with an eye schooled to the appreciation of the beautiful in nature, became impressed with the loveliness of the situation. The gently undulating surface, the groves of magnificent oaks and other trees of the forest, the natural fertility of the soil, the abundant growth of native grasses, the profusion of wild flowers, the crystal lakes, and generally all that could contribute to the composition of a scene of rural beauty and almost absolute enchantment, attracted the attention of Father Badin and became a prophecy, in his mind, of future advantages and pious uses. He, therefore, lost no time in becoming the owner of a magnificent domain, of some eleven hundred acres, and, with a zealous devotion to the Catholic Church, resolved to dedicate it to the education of youth. With him to resolve was to execute. He placed the title in the hands of the ruling authorities of the Church, and in a few years it was transferred to the "right man in the right place," the Very Rev.

E. Sorin, priest of the congregation of the Holy Cross, who, with a few brothers of the same order, had then recently come to America from France. In 1842, Father Sorin, (with his *confreres*,) took possession and with that pious determination and indomitable energy which enter largely into the character of this extraordinary man, he immediately commenced that system of improvements which has, in less than a quarter of a century, resulted in placing "Notre Dame du Lac" very far towards the head of the educational institutions in America.

The "University of Notre Dame" was incorporated by the Legislature of Indiana, in 1844. It is situated on a table of land elevated nearly a hundred feet above the St. Joseph river, and distant from the river and the center of South Bend but a little over one mile. It is on the banks of two lovely lakes of clear, cool spring water. On one hand Arcadian groves of native forest trees, adorned by all the appliances of cultivated art, invite to their cooling shades and silent retreats; on the other a landscape of sylvan beauty, rarely surpassed, stretches as far as the eye can reach. The college is of most liberal proportions, and of that subdued, though tasteful style of architecture, eminently fitted for its uses. An air of quietude and neatness pervades every part, not only of the college but of the whole domain. It is conducted by the Fathers of the Congregation of the Holy Cross, assisted by a number of competent lay professors in the various branches of study. The whole is very ably presided over by the Rev. W. Corby, Father Superior. These educators, with a profound appreciation of the keynotes of the human mind, have successfully elaborated and, with admirable tact and ability, now conduct an institution which is not only valuable but attractive. Here is no rude coercion, no fear of punishment, no abnegation of individualism, but all are kept within the line of duty by a noble sense of honor and justice. A healthy emulation is excited by various devices which appeal to the higher and nobler faculties of the youthful mind.

The University has recently, in addition to the land above spoken of, purchased a tract of about thirteen hundred acres in Harris township, and they also own a fine peat bed on the Kankakee, which they have commenced working. A trial of this peat shows it to be superior in every respect, as fuel, to the best wood.

Some idea of the magnitude of this educational establishment may be gathered from the fact that there are annually consumed there and at St. Mary's Academy, four hundred and fifty beef cattle, one thousand fat sheep, sixty thousand pounds of pork, seven thousand bushels of wheat, and other articles in proportion.

The Northern Indiana College is located at South Bend, at the west end of Washington street, just one mile from the court house. Its position is easy of access, healthy, and affords a fine view of the city and surrounding country.

The Northern Indiana College was founded in 1861, by an association of protestant gentlemen, residing at and in the vicinity of South Bend. They organized under the act of the General Assembly, entitled an act for the incorporation of High Schools, Academies, Colleges, etc.—and the purpose of the association is described in the following extract from the records, to wit:

"To establish an Institution of learning, for the education of both male and female students, in the various branches of the arts and sciences usually taught in other Colleges." The first board of trustees was composed of the following named gentlemen, viz: Schuyler Colfax, William Miller, John H. Harper, John Brownfield, Ashbury Clark, George F. Layton, Francis R. Tutt, John W. Chess and Elisha Egbert. Like most institutions of the kind in our young country, it has had many difficulties to contend with, principally of a financial character. On this account the edifice was not fully completed until the fall of 1866, soon after which, it was consecrated to the sacred cause of science, by appropriate services, conducted by Rev. Dr. Eddy, of Chicago.

The College building does honor to its projectors, and is an ornament to the city with which it is connected. It is built of brick, fifty by ninety feet and four stories high including basement. The front is ornamented by a central and cylindrical tower, rising to an altitude of nearly one hundred feet, and connected with every floor in the building. The interior arrangement is well adapted to educational purposes, and the whole edifice finished in a workmanlike manner. Young ladies are accommodated with pleasant, well ventilated rooms, in the college building, and young gentlemen may be furnished with board, or room to board themselves, in the immediate neighborhood. Students who come here to pursue their studies will find competent and experienced teachers in every department. Study rooms, recitation rooms, society rooms, a library and reading room, maps and apparatus for illustrating the principles of natural science. The boarding hall is under the superintendence of Rev. James Johnson and lady, well and favorably known in this section of country. The school is under the governmental and educational control of the M. E. Church, yet is conducted on liberal and unsectarian principles. The college is now in running order, and needs only an increased share of public patronage to make it a success.

All denominations of christians and the public generally are invited to enjoy the facilities here afforded for the education of their sons and daughters.

The fall session for 1867, opened on the first Wednesday in September. The President of this Institution is Rev. D. Holmes, D. D., a gentleman who has few equals and no superiors as an educator. He is assisted by a competent faculty. The Northern Indiana College, though young and just emerging from the varied difficulties incident to new enterprises of the kind, has already entered upon a sphere of usefulness which will ultimate in most beneficient results. It has a noble future in prospect, and the day is coming when the gentlemen who have made large sacrifices in its foundation will be held in most affectionate remembrance by a matured generation of intelligent, useful and christian men and women. It is most heartily commended to the patronage of the St. Joseph Valley particularly and to Indiana and the whole country in general.

St. Mary's Academy, under the direction of the sisters of the Holy Cross, and devoted to the education of females, is pleasantly situated upon the east bank of the St. Joseph river, not far from one mile below South Bend. This is exclusively a boarding school. It has already earned for itself a high reputation and as a consequence is very liberally patronised, both by Catholics and Protestants. The buildings are large and well adapted to the purposes for which they were constructed. Hot and cold baths attached to the sleeping apartments form a peculiarity which may well be copied elsewhere. Only one wing of the edifice, as it is designed to be, has been yet erected. There is ample accommodation for several hundred pupils. It has just entered upon its twelfth year of usefulness. All branches of a liberal female education are taught, including vocal and instrumental music and the modern languages. Its proximity to Notre Dame, it being less than a mile distant, is a great convenience to parents having children at both institutions.

St. Joseph Academy is an institution for the education of females, and is situated in the city of South Bend. It is an elegant edifice of large proportions, and is under the management of the sisters of the Holy Cross. This school is intended for the accommodation of externs, or day scholars, in which it differs entirely from St. Mary's, where only boarders are taken. It has been in operation only about two years, but has already won a large share of public favor.

St. Patrick's Select School is situated in South Bend, contiguous to the church of the same name. It is a Catholic school, of the parochial order, and not incorporated. It was organized in 1866, by the present principal, Rev. P. P. Cooney. It is intended for boys. This school is in a thriving condition, and enjoys a substantial patronage.

A Spencerian Commercial College has been for some time in successful operation at South Bend. It is pleasantly and airily located on the corner of Main and Washington streets, and is ably managed by its enterprising conductors, Messrs. Sumption and Adams. These gentlemen also preside over a select graded school at the same place, which has thus far proved a success and a blessing. Mr. Sumption has been for many years actively engaged in the profession, and as a teacher, has the confidence of all who know him. He is now the Examiner of the schools of St. Joseph county.

A good public school is kept up in each ward of the city during several months of each year.

We had intended to give a brief history of the press of the valley, but the task proves to be so difficult and the labor so great that the purpose has been abandoned. We shall, however, undertake to make a connected statement of the papers hitherto and presently published in South Bend, as we have already done in reference to some other places.

The publication of the *Northwestern Pioneer* was commenced at South Bend, in October, 1831, by John D. Defrees and his brother Joseph H. Defrees. The former of these gentlemen has since occupied many positions of trust and honor—has been a member of Congress, and is now the able Superintendent of Public Printing at Washington. The latter is an esteemed citizen of Goshen, in Elkhart county. The *Pioneer*, be it remembered, was the *first newspaper ever published north of Logansport and west of Detroit.* Chicago was then an uninhabited morass, and all beyond *terra incognita.* At the end of six months the *Pioneer* was changed to the *St. Joseph Beacon.* In 1833, John D. Defrees bought his brother's interest and removed the office to White Pigeon, Michigan, and shortly afterwards sold it to a man by the name of Gilbert.

The *South Bend Free Press* was started by William Millikan about 1836, and was published until 1845, when it was changed to the *St. Joseph Valley Register*, and came under the editorial management of Hon. Schuyler Colfax, the present distinguished Speaker of the House of Representatives. Mr. Colfax was not a printer, as many have supposed, but was a very able editor and a safe business man. In 1854 Mr. Alfred Wheeler became associated with Mr. Colfax. In 1855 the whole interest passed into the hands of Mr. Wheeler, who continued the publication up to 1866, when he sold out to Archibald Beal and C. E. Fuller, the present publishers. The *Register* has enjoyed a large circulation for many years and has occupied a wide field of influence and usefulness. Mr. Millikan is now editor of the *Fayette County Herald*, published at Washington, Ohio.

In 1844, Thomas Jernigan published the *Mishawaka Tocsin*, and removed the office to South Bend, where Jernigan & Harris resumed its publication under the name of the *Indiana Tocsin.* In 1845 the *Tocsin* was removed to Laporte and was there published under another name. Mr. Jernigan now resides in Michigan City, where he edits a paper and holds a federal office.

In 1848 W. R. Ellis published a paper called the *Free Democrat.* It was devoted to the support of the free soil party and of Martin VanBuren for the presidency. It survived but a few month. Mr. Ellis now lives in Lafayette, Indiana.

The *St. Joseph County Forum* was established in 1853, by A. E. Drapier and his son Wm. H. Drapier. This was the first democratic paper published in South Bend. The elder Drapier retired after a year or two and left the paper in the hands of his son who, after being connected with it thirteen years to a day, sold the establishment to an association of democratic gentlemen in 1866. On the occasion of the change of proprietors the name was dropped, and it is now published by Mr. E. Molloy as the *National Union*. The *Forum* was for some months, at one time, issued semi-weekly, but the experiment was not a financial success.

There is now published a monthly periodical at Notre Dame called *Ave Maria*. It is a religious publication, devoted to the interests of the Catholic Church, and has a wide circulation among persons of that faith.

New Carisle is a flourishing town, on the Northern Indiana Railroad, fourteen miles west of South Bend. It is located on an abrupt elevation of land overlooking Terre Coupee prairie. The situation is a very desirable and commanding one. The population does not vary much from five hundred. At this place the Methodists have established the Carlisle Collegiate Institute, a school for the education of both sexes. This Institute has already taken a high position among the many classical schools of Northern Indiana. The building is of brick, and is commodious and convenient, while all its surroundings are beautiful and inviting. The sexes are educated together, and on a perfect equality. Its existence, so far, has been marked with great success, and a brilliant future seems to be within its reach. Isaac W. McCasky, A. M., is president, and he is assisted by a full corps of teachers in the various English, classical and ornamental branches. The place is healthy and retired, yet easy of access; and students enjoy, in addition to other advantages, the benefit of quiet, intelligent and refined society.

New Carlisle is not properly in the St. Joseph Valley, but its interests are so closely associated with South Bend and St. Joseph county, that we have not felt at liberty to omit mentioning it.

6

BERRIEN COUNTY, MICHIGAN.

This is the extreme southwestern county of the State. It is, on its northwesterly side, for many miles, washed by the waters of Lake Michigan. The equable and moderate climate occasioned by proximity to the lake, and the peculiar quality of the soil, render a large portion of the county celebrated as a fruit growing region. Apples, pears and peaches here grow in luscious perfection, and in large quantities, so that had the county no other resources it would soon become populous and wealthy from fruit-growing alone. Peaches, especially, all along the shore of, and for many miles back from, the lake are produced in great abundance and of a very superior quality, and the excellent facilities for transportation afforded by water and railroad to the great markets east and west, give to this fruit a value which must always make its culture very profitable. The peach crop here is never known to fail entirely, as in most other places, but its quantity seldom has any limit except the ability of the trees to carry their burthen of fruit. Indeed, so certain is it, that it is not uncommon for the prospective products of whole orchards to be contracted for, in the lump, before the appearance of a single blossom. The quality of this fruit is excellent, and in all accessible markets it commands the highest price. All kinds of small fruits are here abundantly and profitably cultivated. But Berrien county is not alone adapted to fruit-raising; it is also one of the best sections of Michigan for general agriculture. Wheat, corn and grass appear to be both protected and stimulated by the climatic influence of the neighboring lake. The general surface is rolling, but scarcely ever broken. There are some small prairies, but only a few marshes. The oak openings are extensive, but forests of pine, oak, walnut, poplar, beech, maple, and other trees, abound. A large amount of capital is employed in the manufacture of lumber for export; and like many other sections of our country, the land is likely to be soon denuded of its wealth of lumber. Cupidity and waste have joined hands in this unpardonable and irreparable destruction. Under the shadow of private right this public wrong is safely perpetrated, and no one has power to prevent or restrain it. The man who now destroys the most timber, by cutting it into lumber, is said to be the most enterprising; posterity will, very properly, pronounce him to have been the greatest nuisance of his day. The wanton, careless or useless felling of a tree, ought to be considered a great crime; and the man who, for mere gain, strips his farm of those beautiful forests which nature has planted, should be sent to the asylum for the insane or for idiots.

The St. Joseph river enters the county in the township of Bertrand, and runs in a generally north direction, through Niles, Buchanan and Berrien Springs, to St. Joseph, where it empties into Lake Michigan. At the city of Niles it receives the water of the Dowagiac river, and a short distance above its mouth the Paw Paw falls into it. Both these streams afford many and fine mill sites, and the hydraulic capacity of the St. Joseph constantly increases as it sweeps through the county. Galien river, Pipestone, McCoy's, Hickory, Yellow and Blue creeks, drain and water other parts of the county, and furnish a large amount of water power.

The history of Berrien county is somewhat peculiar and very interesting, and ought to be written at large. We are happy to be able to state that this duty will soon be accomplished by Hon. Nathaniel Bacon, of Niles, who is now preparing, and will, at an early day, publish a very full history of the St. Joseph Valley. The known ability of Judge Bacon, together with the industry and perseverance with which he has sought and examined all available sources of information, warrant the expectation that he will present a very interesting and useful book. Here it was that, nearly two hundred years ago, the great explorer LaSalle, with Hennepin and Tonti, first discovered the mouth of our beautiful St. Joseph river; here, on the borders of the lake, these forerunners of a Christian civilization built a fort; here, at that early day, the voice of praise and prayer ascended to the "unknown God" of the aborigines; and here the first white man boldly pushed his prow into the solitude of this then unexplored valley. Here, also, were early missions established, councils held and treaties made with the Indian tribes; here was the first orchard planted west of Detroit, and here, to-day, a cross marks the grave of the first white man who died in the valley. And then the events of modern years, though more numerous, are not less interesting. How the first settlers and settlements sped; their struggles, sufferings and successes; the growth of improvements, towns and cities; the establishment of civil, religious and social institutions; the development of material resources; the departure of the aborigines; life in the camp and in the cabin, and the transition to more æsthetic abodes; all this and much more, form a theme most inviting to the philosophic thinker or to the intelligent historian.

The first permanent settlement in this county was made by John Johnson, in 1827, although as early as 1820 there had been an Indian trading post established. In 1840 the population was about 5,000, and twenty years thereafter it had reached 22,274. It is now, probably, over 30,000. In 1860 the cereals produced in the county were as follows:

Wheat,	260,000	bushels.
Rye,	26,000	"
Corn,	456,000	"
Oats,	75,000	"

A large proportion of the emigration into this as into most of the other counties in Southern Michigan, has been from New England and New York. This fact accounts for the high degree of perfection to which the common schools have there been brought. The first public improvement a New England man looks to in a new country is a school house, and until this is completed and in use he does not begin to feel at home. This he knows to be the foundation for other and higher schools, the sure precursor of academies, seminaries and colleges. The common school is his pet; and the better it is the greater is his satisfaction. For it his money, however laboriously earned, goes freely. He looks upon it with the pride of a prince, and when he sees his children marching, in cleanly attire, to this rudimental temple of learning, he glows with that self-satisfied importance which only the true-hearted *pater familias* can feel. It is not, therefore, strange that Berrien county rejoices in the superiority of her common schools. No better exist anywhere; and in addition to them she has also several institutions of what are claimed to be a higher grade. The Union school at Niles is equal to any in the nation, and is one of the chief ornaments of that city, both in a material and a higher sense. In 1860 there were 6,220 pupils in daily attendance at the several public schools of the county. This number has since been largely increased. To this fact may be attributed the general intelligence of the people, and also the good judgment recently displayed in electing so capable and suitable a gentleman as Captain Henry A. Ford to superintend the affairs of these "colleges of the poor man."

About six miles below South Bend we cross the boundary line between Indiana and Michigan, and immediately come to Bertrand, a village which reminds the observer of "the last rose of summer." There was a time, many years ago, when Bertrand was a town of much promise. It had its wide and long streets, its public squares, and its church sites—nearly all in the woods. The territorial road crossed the river here, and the town enjoyed considerable trade. Corner lots were plenty, and amazingly high; indeed, so high that nobody would buy them. And so it died—died of wounds received in the house of its friends. It is now a place of no importance, and has but about three hundred inhabitants.

The city of Niles is situated on the St. Joseph river at its confluence with the Dowagiac. It is the commercial and manufacturing center of the county, and a place of large importance in the State. The first settlement was made in 1827. The plat of the town was made in 1829, and it became an incorporated village in 1834. In 1859 it was incorporated as a city. The name is derived from the editor of the celebrated *Niles' Register*. The first store was opened in 1830, and the first church (Presbyterian) was built in 1833. The city in 1860 had 2,826 inhabitants, but its growth since then has been rapid, and it probably has now considerably over 5,000. Niles is handsomely laid out on both sides of the St. Joseph river, which is here spanned by two bridges. There are many very beautiful locations for private residence, some of which are improved with good taste. The business houses are generally large, substantial and convenient. The Union School House is a very fine building, and in point of architectural beauty and general effect surpasses all other buildings in the city. It has accommodations for over twelve hundred scholars, and is surrounded by grounds very prettily laid out. There are several manufactories here, among which may be mentioned five flouring and two saw mills, a foundry and a machine shop. The machinery is driven by the Dowagiac, which furnishes a fine water power. Several attempts have been made to build a dam across the St. Joseph river, but for some reason they have been unsuccessful. At the present time a hydraulic company with ample means and becoming energy are repeating the attempt, and will, without doubt, accomplish the work. There is no impediment to the construction of a dam at Niles which does not exist at all other places where such an improvement has stood for years. The water power is here too valuable to allow slight discouragements to control. The citizens of Niles are proud of their city; they aim high, and are not made to be beat by water—it will take something stronger to do it. On this power the city depends for its future rapid and permanent growth. Without it, Niles may be considered one of the finished cities; with it, no one can predict any limit to its business, wealth, population and importance. No town in the valley which depends alone, or chiefly, upon local trade for its prosperity, can attain to any enviable proportions. Niles is no exception; and unless she uses the great advantages which nature has provided, and builds up a manufacturing business, she will see other towns sweeping by, and leaving her to mourn over her folly and her fate.

The village of BUCHANAN, at the mouth of McCoy's creek, a few miles below Niles, has a population of over a thousand. It has two newspapers, several churches, two flouring mills, and some other manufactories. It is a brisk town, handsomely situated, and has a good local trade.

BERRIEN SPRINGS is the capital of the county. It occupies the site of an old French fort on the St. Joseph river, some ten miles below Niles, and fifteen miles from the mouth of the river. Its only means of communication with the outer world is by stage and steamboat. It is innocent of railroads, which accounts for the fact that, although very pleasantly located and enjoying many great natural advantages, it has only about a thousand people. This cannot remain so long. A railroad from the mouth of the river, by the way of Berrien Springs and Niles, to South Bend, is not only contemplated, but its completion is certain at a very early day. The road can be easily and cheaply made, and will be highly important to the country and towns through which it will pass. This improvement accomplished, and Berrien Springs will soon become important for something else besides being the depository of the county records, and as a place to which the judges of the courts and a few lawyers make periodical but flying visits. The name of the village is suggestive of a natural means of wealth, near by, which may, even before long, make the place famous as a delightful resort for health and pleasure. We refer to the numerous mineral springs. There are found here several very fine white sulphur springs, and some other mineral waters, whose qualities deserve further analysis. The region is evidently volcanic, and some persons are decidedly of the opinion that they have found unmistakable evidences of oil—a slander upon the locality which we have no idea will ever be verified. These mineral waters are of such a character and quantity as to lead to the expectation that, before many years, a great watering place will be established here. A recent writer, referring to this town, says it is "beautifully situated, healthily located, with a fine chalybeate spring within the corporation, and a sulphur spring on the opposite side of the river, and surrounded by fine farms; overlooking the beautiful St. Joseph, in sight of majestic woods, and in the center of the great fruit region of Western Michigan, it could not fail to be a charming resort. Just above the town are the beautifully embowered Indian Fields, still retaining the footmarks of barbaric life, even now much frequented. Opposite is Fruit Island No. 1, an island garden, bordered with majestic trees and embowered with climbing vines. Below and opposite the main mineral springs and basin are the celebrated Shaker farms and establishment. The river, both above and below the village, is a thing of beauty, bordered and embowered with the sycamore, black walnut, buckeye, pawpaw and wild grape; and as a place for rambles, walks and drives, is unsurpassed for romantic loveliness and sylvan beauty. Peaches, apples, grapes, sweet potatoes, and all kinds of berries, wild and tame; fish in the river and game in the woods largely abound."

At the mouth of the St. Joseph river and at the terminus of the Valley, is situated the village of ST. JOSEPH, a thriving town of about twenty-five hundred inhabitants. Here the Paw Paw falls into the St. Joseph, and here, also, is one of the best and most commodious harbors on Lake Michigan. It has a fine local trade, and ships large quantities of lumber, grain and fruit. A line of propellers furnishes daily communication with Chicago, and the interior is reached by steamboat and stage. The country all along the lake, and for several miles back, is specially adapted to the culture of fruit, and has the appearance of being almost one continuous peach orchard. This is the point at which LaSalle with his retinue of explorers landed, when he discovered the mouth of the river. Here he built a fort, over which floated the flag of France, and here the cross was first displayed to the wondering gaze of the aborigines of the valley. A railroad up the St. Joseph river to connect with the two great east and west lines, and making a continuous route to the Ohio river, will very suddenly increase the importance of the town and the harbor.

CONCLUSION.

We have thus briefly gone over the proposed ground, following the river from its source to its mouth, and occasionally making diversions toward the borders of the valley. Of course the view which we have taken has been limited and imperfect. Our first purpose has been to exhibit, as fully as possible, the wonderful hydraulic capacity of the valley, and to sketch some of the great business advantages. Even this we have but imperfectly done; yet we think enough has been presented to arrest the attention of the reader, and to stimulate a personal examination by those who are seeking locations for business or homes. From one end to the other of the valley there are numerous inducements for settlement. The climate is genial and equable; the water is abundant and pure; land is cheap and productive; timber is plenty; roads are good; schools are excellent, and society intelligent and refined. No branch of industry is over-done, and good homes, cheap subsistence, and ample fortunes are sure to reward persevering and well-directed labor. If the foregoing pages serve to give direction to even a small portion of those who are seeking new homes and opportunities for usefulness, and assist in developing, in some degree, the dormant capabilities of the lovely Valley of the St. Joseph, the object of the writer will have been substantially attained.

OFFICERS OF ST. JOSEPH COUNTY, INDIANA.

Auditor—W. J. Holloway.
Treasurer—Ezekiel Green.
Clerk—E. V. Clark.
Recorder—R. J. Chestnutwood.
Sheriff—Sol. W. Palmer.
Commissioners—Gilman Towle, J. C. Knoblock, Nathaniel Frame.

COURTS.

Circuit Court—First Mondays of March and September. Hon. Andrew J. Osborn, Judge.

Court of Common Pleas—Third Mondays of January, May and September. Hon. Elisha Egbert, Judge.

ST. JOSEPH COUNTY AGRICULTURAL SOCIETY.

President—William F. Bulla.
Vice President—Nathaniel Frame.
Treasurer—William Miller.
Secretary—Charles Towle.

JUSTICES OF THE PEACE, SOUTH BEND.

Benjamin Wall,
William H. Stanfield,
Jacob Hardman.

OFFICERS OF THE

INDIANA STATE BOARD OF AGRICULTURE.

President—Hon. A. D. Hamrick..Hamrick's Station, Putnam Co.
Vice President—Dr. John C. Helm........Muncie, Delaware Co.
Treasurer—Carlos Dickson.......................Indianapolis.
General Superintendent—John B. Sullivan..........Indianapolis.
Secretary—A. J. Holmes.................Rochester, Fulton Co.
(*Office*—State House, Indianapolis.)

EXECUTIVE COMMITTEE.

Hon. A. D. Hamrick, President, *Ex-officio.*
Hon. W. C. Danaldson, Hon. James D. Williams,
J. A. Grosvenor, Joseph Poole.

MEMBERS OF THE STATE BOARD OF AGRICULTURE.

1*st District*—E. T. Cox..............New Harmony, Posey Co.
2*d District*—Hon. J. D. Williams..Pond Creek Mills, Knox Co.
3*d District*—John C. Shoemaker..............Rome, Perry Co.
4*th District*—John McCrea.......................Bloomington.
5*th District*—Benjamin North....................Rising Sun.
6*th District*—D. E. Rees ....Lawrenceburg.
7*th District*—J. A. Grosvenor...................Indianapolis.
8*th District*—Hon. W. C. Danaldson.....Montezuma, Parke Co,
9*th District*—Hon. A. D. Hamrick ....Putnam Co.
10*th District*—Alexander Heron..................Connorsville
11*th District*—Dr. John C. Helm.......................Muncie.
12*th District*—Joseph Poole ....Attica, Fountain Co.
13*th District*—Hezekiah Caldwell ....Wabash.
14*th District*—A. J. Holmes........................Rochester.
15*th District*—John Sutherland ....Laporte.
16*th District*—Dr. George W. McConnell..............Angola.

CITY OF SOUTH BEND, INDIANA.

The Post Office of South Bend is situated on the corner of Main and Market streets. Edwin R. Farnum is postmaster.

The city government of South Bend is composed as follows:

Mayor—William E. George.
Councilmen—1st Ward: John Klingle, S. F. Myers.
2d Ward: Thos. S. Stanfield, David Stover.
3d Ward: Thos. W. Defrees, A. B. Merrett.
4th Ward: A. Russworm, S. Parry.
Clerk—John Hagerty.
Marshall—Jacob K. Huston.
Street Commissioner—John A. Hartman.
City Engineer—Mathias Stover.
Chief of Fire Department—John Brownfield.
City Attorney—Geo. Pfleger, Jr.
Treasurer—J. B. Eaker.

FIRE DEPARTMENT.

Chief Engineer—John Brownfield.
1*st Assistant Engineer*—Nathan Marsh.
2*d* " " William Mack.

Engine Company, No. 1—E. P. Taylor, Foreman.
" " " 2—Benjamin White, Foreman.
Hook and Ladder Co.—John Brownfield, Foreman.

The Masonic Organizations in South Bend are as follows:

ST. JOSEPH LODGE No. 45.

[Instituted in 1842.]

W. M.—George H. Alward.
S. W.—Theodore Witherell.
J. W.—Israel Belton.
Treas.—Dwight Deming.
Secy.—M. A. Smith.
S. D.—W. F. Cushing.
J. D.—Ed. Turnock.

SOUTH BEND LODGE No. 294.

[Instituted in 1863.]

W. M.—O. H. Brusie.
S. W.—Archibald Defrees.
J. W.—Joseph Henderson.
Treas.—Adam Barnhart.
Secy.—C. Souders.

GERMANIA LODGE No. 301.

[Instituted in 1865.]

W. M.—John Klingle.
S. W.—M. Livingston.
J. W.—Charles Vinson.
Treas.—Jacob Myers.
Secy.—John Meussel.
S. D.—John Zeitler.
J. D.—Leonard Bock.
Stewards.—Herman Yonker, Gerard Berger.
Tyler.—Andrew Russworm.

The Odd Fellows organizations are as follows:

SOUTH BEND LODGE No. 29.

[Instituted in 1846.]

N. G.—C. Studebaker.
V. G.—M. L. Huey.
Secy.—J. G. Vinson.
Treas.—John Gallagher.

SOUTH BEND ENCAMPMENT I. O. O. F.

[Instituted in 1848.]

C. P.—W. J. Holloway.
H. P.—S. W. Palmer.
S. W.—V. G. Huey.
J. W.—William Miller.
S.—A. Wheeler.
Treas.—C. W. Martin.

ROBERT BLUM LODGE.

[Instituted in 1867.]

N. G.—J. G. Vinson.
V. G.—G. Poehlman.
Secy.—John Wagner.
Treas.—Frederick Grether.

GOOD TEMPLARS.

GUIDING STAR LODGE No. 371.

[Instituted in 1866.]

W. C. T.—E. B. Metzger.
W. V. T.—Miss Jennie Eaker.
W. S.—James R. Davis.
W. F. S.—Almon Bugbee.
W. T.—Miss Mattie Bulla.
W. M.—Marion Staley.
W. D. M.—Miss Ritter.
W. I. G.—Miss Alena Rees.
W. O. G.—Washington Saunders.
W. A. S.—Willis Bugbee.
W. R. H. S.—Miss Lucretia Miller.
W. L. H. S.—Miss Ritter.
W. Chaplin—Elder Israel Beldon.
P. W. C. T.—Corydon E. Fuller.

YOUNG MEN'S ASSOCIATION.

[Instituted in 1866.]

President—Robert Johnson.
Vice President—J. A. M. LaPierre.
Cor. Secretary--Wm. S. Bartlett.
Rec. Secretary—Washington Saunders.
Treasurer—Alexander Ireland.

GRAND ARMY OF THE REPBLIC.

SOUTH BEND POST.

P. C.—Alexander N. Thomas.
Sen. P. C.- -Daniel Dayton.
Jun. P. C.—Ed. Nicar.
Adjutant—William Stover.
Q. M.—D. Smith.
Surgeon.—Dr. S. F. Myers.
Chaplain.—L. G. Welton.

CHURCHES IN SOUTH BEND.

Methodist Episcopal—North-west corner of Main and Jefferson streets. Rev. ———— , pastor.

Methodist Episcopal—(German,)—Lafayette street, between Washington and Jefferson.

Presbyterian—South-west corner Washington and Lafayette streets. Rev. Walter Forsythe, pastor.

Baptist—South-east corner Main and Jefferson streets. Rev. Thomas P. Campbell, pastor.

Reformed Dutch—South-west corner Lafayette and Market streets.

Lutheran—South-west corner Lafayette and Market streets. Rev. Phillip Wagner, pastor. Worship in the Reformed Dutch Church.

Roman Catholic—(St. Patrick's,)—Division, between Scott and Chapin streets. Rev. P. P. Cooney, priest.

Universalist—Main, between Washington and Jefferson streets. Rev. Nathaniel Crary, pastor.

Disciples of Christ—Main, between Wayne and Division streets. Rev. Israel Belton, pastor.

ST. JOSEPH VALLEY REGISTER

NEWSPAPER,

BOOK AND JOB PRINTING

AND

BOOK BINDING ESTABLISHMENT,

A. BEAL & CO., Proprietors,

No. 86 MICHIGAN STREET,

SOUTH BEND, - - - INDIANA.

THE REGISTER,

Established in 1845, by Hon. SCUYLER COLFAX, has much the largest circulation of any paper in Northern Indiana, and is, therefore, an excellent **MEDIUM FOR ADVERTISING.**

Subscriptions $2.00 per year in advance. Advertising rates reasonable.

JOB PRINTING.

The Register Job Office is well supplied with Power Presses and material for excuting all kinds of **JOB PRINTING** in the best style; and is daily turning out work equal to the best offices in the large cities and at much lower prices.

BOOK BINDING.

The Register Bindery is now in successful operation. All kinds of work executed in good style and at reasonable prices. A first class Ruling Machine is connected with the Bindery, and the various styles of BLANK WORK will be neatly and promptly executed.

Orders from a distance for Job Printing, Binding, Ruling, etc., are solicited and satisfaction in all cases will be guaranteed.

NORTHERN INDIANA COLLEGE

MALE AND FEMALE.

WEST END OF WASHINGTON ST., SOUTH BEND, INDIANA.

FACULTY.

President—D. Holmes, A. M., D. D., assisted by five Department Teachers.

OFFICERS OF THE BOARD.

Rev. John Thrush, Pres. F. B. Tutt, Esq., Vice President. A. Beal, Esq., Secretary. John Brownfield, Esq., Treasurer.

CALENDAR FOR 1867 & 1868.

College Year is divided into two sessions of 20 weeks each. First session opens Wednesday, September 4th, 1867. Second session will begin Tuesday, February 4th, 1868; one week's vacation during holidays. Students may enter at any time.

The Boarding Department, within the college building, is intended for the special accommodation of young ladies. It is under the management of Rev. James Johnson and Lady, the latter having the position of Matron. The facilities of this department are equal to those of any similiar institution.

EXPENSES.

Board in College Building with use of room per week,	$3 00.
Light and Fuel will be an extra charge, in no case to exceed per week,...........................	1 00.
Washing per dozen,..............................	60.
Janitor's Fee, per term,..............................	1 00.

TUITION, PER TERM.

Minimum Department,..............................	$4 00.
Medium, First Year,..............................	5 00.
Medium, Second Year,..............................	6 00.
Collegiate and Classical, according to grade of studies,	7 00 to 10 00.
Instrumental Music, including use of Instrument,....	12 00.
Modern Languages, each..............................	5 00.
Painting and Drawing,........................	4 00 to 6 00.

Janitor's Fee must be paid when the name is enrolled, Tuition in advance. In cases of serious illness a deduction will be made, corresponding to time loss. Each Boarding Student is expected to furnish one half the bedding for one bed, except the straw mattress, two students occupying one room. Students will be required to furnish towels, napkins and toilet for their own use.

☞ For further information address the President of the institution, or the Secretary of the Board of Trustees, at South Bend, Indiana.

THE NATIONAL UNION,

A WEEKLY JOURNAL,

PUBLISHED EVERY SATURDAY.

Office in Washington Block, (third Story,)

SOUTH BEND, IND.

The UNION is striving to become the best local paper in Northern Indiana. For that purpose unusual attention is devoted to everything pertaining to South Bend and St. Joseph county. It will always endeavor to maintain Democratic principles, using nothing but argument in attacking or replying to opponents.

Selections of poetry and prose are always made with a strict regard to the highest order of taste; and morality will be firmly defended. No parent need hesitate about allowing the UNION to be perused by the youngest members of his household.

TERMS OF SUBSCRIPTION:

For One year, (in advance,)	$2.00
For Six months, "	1.25
For Three months, "	75

JOB PRINTING.

CARDS,

LETTER HEADS,

CIRCULARS, and

BLANKS,

of all kinds done to order, on short notice.

We do plain and fancy Printing, having on hand a good assortment of metal and wood type.

☞ Our prices are reasonable, being on the "live and let live" order.

Communications on business, or enclosing subscriptions, should be addressed to

E. MOLLOY & Co.,
South Bend, Indiana.

J. W. RUGGLES,

TEACHER OF

Vocal and Instrumental Music

— OF THE —

NORTHERN INDIANA COLLEGE,

SOUTH BEND, IND.

OFFICE AND MUSIC ROOM IN THE CITY,

Room No. 1, Second Floor, St. Joseph Block, on Washington Street, Directly Opposite the Court House.

In the **Vocal Department** I call special attention to the cultivation of the voice, in private lessons and classes; embracing the delivery and registering of the voice; accurate formation of tones and appropriate expression. This is attended to with the greatest care, and in accordance with the practice of the best teachers of the country, among whom are G. F. Root, C. Bassini, and others.

In the **Instrumental Department** I am prepared to give instruction upon the Piano, Organ, Melodeon and Guitar. In either of the branches of Instrumental Music I claim a thorough presentation of the principles of music, and use as text books for the Piano, G. F. Root's unequalled "Curriculum," the most thorough and progressive course ever offered to the musical world. After completing this work, the advanced studies of Listz, Chopin and others will be used when required. For the Organ, Johnson's improved Thorough Bass and Harmony combined, in connection with Rink's Voluntaries and Instructions in Pedal Harmony, etc. For the Guitar, Carcassi's Method, which is progressive and thorough in all its parts.

PIANOS, MELODEONS AND ORGANS

Furnished to customers at lowest retail rates, and none but good articles sold. Every instrument warranted for five years.

Having had ten years experience in the sale of instruments and having been engaged in manufacturing, tuning and repairing a large portion of the time, I thoroughly understand every part of all kinds of musical instruments in use in this country, and will tune or repair such and guarantee satisfaction. Especial attention given to tuning and repairing Pianos. New strings constantly on hand and will be furnished on order. Terms for tuning Pianos in the city:

Single tuning	$3.00
Two tunings per year	5.00
Three " "	6.00
Cleaning Pianos	1.00
Re-covering Hammers, according to materal nsed	$15.00 to 25.00

Old Pianos taken in exchange for new ones at reasonable rates. For further particulars call at my rooms in the St. Joseph Block, or N. I. College.

South Bend, Sept., 1867. J. W. RUGGLES.

SHIVELY'S HALL,

FRONTING ON MICHIGAN STREET,

SOUTH BEND, IND.

This is one of the largest, most convenient and best Halls in Northern Indiana. It is centrally located, and elegantly fitted up for

Theatrical Performances,

Concerts,

Lectures,

and all other purposes requiring ample room and good conveniences. Terms moderate. Apply personally or by letter to

D. M. SHIVELY, Proprietor,
South Bend, Indiana.

JOB PRINTING!

B. F. MILLER & SON,

ST. JOSEPH BLOCK, SOUTH BEND, IND.

Handbills,

Posters,

Programmes,

Cards,

Book Work,

and all kinds of Plain and Ornamental Printing, neatly and promptly done. New Type, new Presses and new Material. All work warranted to give perfect satisfaction.

NICAR, DEMING & CO.

WHOLESALE AND RETAIL DEALERS IN ALL KINDS OF

HARDWARE,

Stoves and Tinware,

Always on hand and for sale at the very lowest figures,
Iron, Steel, Nails, Glass, Putty, Paints, Oils, Brushes and all kinds of Building Hardware. Also,

AGRICULTURAL IMPLEMENTS,

Cooper and Carpenter's Tools,

Leather and Rubber Belting,

CIRCULAR, MILL AND CROSS CUT SAWS, ROPES AND CORDAGE, CUTLERY, GLUE, &c.

All kinds of Tinwork made to order.

AGENT'S FOR THE "LA BELLE," NAIL WORKS,
WHEELING, WEST VIRGINIA.

Laffel & Baldwin's Union Churns.

Agents for Wm. Mann & Co's Mishawka Pattern Axes. Also, genuine Mishawaka Axes.

Cor. Washington and Michigan Sts., South Bend, Ind.

LIVERY. LIVERY.

IRELAND & GISH,

PROPRIETORS,

Opposite the St. Joseph Block, and one door west of the Court House,

SOUTH BEND, INDIANA.

We spare no pains or expense, to keep always for the use of our customers and the public generally,

THE BEST HORSES & BUGGIES

And the most elegant Carriages to be found in the City.

Our Prices are Liberal and our accommodations perfect; in fact, we are determined to give the most perfect satisfaction to all.

SAFE DRIVERS FURNISHED WHEN REQUIRED.

☞ Large wagons on springs, for Parties and Pic-Nics. ☜

HORSES KEPT ON SALE AND BOARDED.

Cash paid for Oats, Corn and Hay.

IRELAND & GISH, South Bend, Ind.

C. LIPHART & CO.

Wholesale and Retail Manufacturers of and Dealers in

All kinds of Furniture,

ON HAND OR MADE TO ORDER,

SOFAS, LOUNGES, CHAIRS, OTTOMANS, CENTER, PARLOR, TEA AND EXTENSION TABLES, BUREAUS, BEDSTEADS, WASH-STANDS, OAK AND WALNUT CHAMBER SETS, LOOKING GLASSES, &c. &c. &c.

COFFINS

Of all prices and kinds constantly on hand.

MICHIGAN ST., South of St. Joseph Co., Bank,

SOUTH BEND, - - INDIANA.

A. COQUILLARD,

LUMBER YARD,

COR. MICHIGAN AND JEFFERSON STS.,

SOUTH BEND, - - INDIANA.

Always on hand and for sale, all kinds and qualities of seasoned Lumber, Shingles, Lath, &c., including Boards, Plank, Scantling, Joists, Flooring, Siding, Fencing, &c.

Cash at all times paid for Walnut, Oak, Ash, Cherry and Poplar Lumber.

Full Bills for Buildings filled without delay and on Accommodating Terms. Call and see.

A. COQUILLARD & CO.

AT THE

CORNER OF LAFAYETTE & WATER STS.,

SOUTH BEND, INDIANA.,

CONTINUE TO MANUFACTURE FOR THE WHOLESALE AND RETAIL TRADE

CARRIAGES, BUGGIES, WAGONS

AND EVERYTHING IN THE VEHICLE LINE

In the greatest variety and of the best materials and with reference to the latest and most approved styles and patterns. We use

MACHINERY OF THE MOST PERFECT KINDS,

And employ none but the most capable and experienced mechanics that can be procured, in the various branches of our business.

OUR TIMBER IS THOROUGHLY SEASONED

And all materials are subjected to a RIGID INSPECTION.

The success which has hitherto attended our enterprise we hold as an indication of public satisfaction, and we are determined to abate no effort to maintain the position we have attained.

We have on hand at all times a large stock of articles in our line, which we intend to

SELL AT VERY LOW PRICES,

In fact, in no event will we be UNDERSOLD. Give us a call, or address, by letter, as above, when all information will be given.

CITY LIVERY,

[OPPOSITE DWIGHT HOUSE,]

I. SKINNER, Proprietor,

No. 54 Michigan Street,

SOUTH BEND, - - - INDIANA.

THE BEST OF

Horses, Buggies and Carriages,

At all times, and at reasonable prices.

SALE STABLE.

Horses sold or exchanged on fair terms.

BOARDING.

Horses boarded and taken care of in the best manner and satisfaction guaranteed.

CASH PAID FOR CORN, OATS AND HAY.

I. SKINNER.

NEW YORK CLOTHING STORE,

PALMER'S NEW BUILDING, SOUTH BEND, IND.

Clothing of all kinds at Lowest Rates and of Best Quality.

GENTLEMEN'S FURNISHING GOODS,

Including Collars, Cuffs, Gloves, Hoseries, Handkerchiefs, Shirts, &c., &c. A fine stock of

Cloths, Cassimers and Vestings

Always on hand and made to order.

HATS, CAPS, TRUNKS, SATCHELS, VALISES, ETC.

Our motto is, Good Fits or no sale. None but the best workmen employed. Give us a call.

LANTZ BRO'S & CO.

GEO. F. LAYTON,

DRUGGIST AND APOTHECARY,

[REGISTER BUILDING,]

No. 86 Michigan Street, South Bend, Ind.

Offers to the public a large and well selected stock of Drugs, Chemicals, Dye Stuffs, Druggists' Sundries, Proprietary Medicines, Perfumery, Cosmetics, Hair, Nail and Tooth Brushes, Hair Dyes and Hair Restoratives, all of unrivalled excellence.

LUBRICATING AND BURNING OILS.

Physician's Prescriptions filled with accuracy and despatch at all times *Puritas et Perfectios Probus Parotive.*

LIKEWISE:

BLANK BOOKS, STATIONERY, A Geneneral Assortment, SCHOOL and COLLEGE TEXT BOOKS.

Which will be sold as cheap as at any House in South Bend.

MARSH & MILLER,

Wholesale Manufacturers of

Sash, Doors, Blinds,

MOULDINGS, BRACKETS, &c.,

FACTORY ON THE EAST SIDE SOUTH BEND, IND.

Planing, scroll sawing, and re-sawing of all descriptions done to order. Stair railing, balusters, Newel Posts, on hand or made as required. A large stock of sash, doors, blinds, mouldings and plain and ornamental fence pickets, constantly on hand. Dressed flooring, siding and finishing lumber for sale at all times. In short, everything requisite for finishing a house, can be had of best quality and on short notice, at this establishment.

DWIGHT HOUSE,

SOUTH BEND, INDIANA,

D. DEMING, Proprietor.

This House is first class in all respects. The bedding and furniture are all new, and the rooms neat, airy and commodious. Omnibuses at all the trains, for the Hotel or any part of the city.

Stages leave this house daily for Niles, Berrien and St. Joseph, Michigan.

Express coaches depart for Mishawaka, Notre Dame and St. Mary's, several times each day.

GOOD STABLING.

W. G. GEORGE. GEO. PFLEGER, JR.

GEORGE & PFLEGER,

Attorneys at Law,

OFFICE OVER THE POST OFFICE,

SOUTH BEND, INDIANA.

Practice in the Supreme and Circuit Courts of the State, and in the Federal Courts. Collections Promptly attended to.

George Pfleger, Jr., is Notary Public and Commissioner for the State of Pennsylvania.

REED & COONLEY'S

DRUG STORE,

IN THE NEW BRICK BLOCK,

On the corner of Michigan and Washington Streets.

Fitted up by their superintendence, for them, has long been known to the residents of St. Joseph County, and doing business at South Bend, as one of the best in Northern Indiana.

They claim all goods sold by them to be perfectly pure and strictly as represented. They hope that a close attention to business, and honesty, will secure success. They treat all alike cordially, and wish success to all their numerous friends and customers.

They always have on hand a large and complete stock of Drugs and Medicines, Linseed Oil and White Lead, all kinds of Paints and Painter's Goods. All the standard Patent Medicines of the day, Machine Oil and Fish Oil, Benzine and Turpentine, Varnishes of the best quality, Fruit Jars, Tobacco, Cigars and Pipes. We wish to satisfy all favoring us with a call.

G. S. REED. D. M. COONLEY.

WITHERILL & CO.

DEALERS IN

Clocks, Watches, Jewelry,

Pure Silver and Plated Ware, Books, Stationery, Wall Paper and Window Shades, Watches, Clocks, &c., repaired in the best manner. The latest newspapers and periodicals always on hand

No. 95 MICHIGAN STREET,

NORTH OF WASHINGTON STREET, SOUTH BEND, IND.

JOHN K. SELTZER,

Dealer in all kinds of Groceries, Fruits, Fish, Vegetables, Glass,

Queens and Stone Ware, Teas, Coffee and Sugars. Also, Flour, Meal, and all kinds of feed. Cash paid for Wheat, Corn, Oats, Fruit, and all sorts of country produce, at the

COR. OF WASHINGTON & MICHIGAN STS., South Bend

BULLA & ROSE,

DEALERS IN

HATS, CAPS & FURS,

Paper Collars, Neck Ties, Travelling Bags and Valises,

Gloves and all kinds of Buffalo Robes, &c. Our prices are suited to the times, and to the general truth that "we will not be undersold." Call and see us and we guarantee satisfaction,

92 MICHIGAN ST., *Bet. Market & Washington,*

Next Door to Cushing's Drug Store, South Bend, Indiana.

TREATMENT OF CHRONIC DISEASES BY

Drs. L. PAGIN & BROS.,

NEW SCHOOL PHYSICIANS, SOUTH BEND, IND.

We make no pretentions of ability to cure ALL disease; we leave such arrogant and dishonest assumption to the horde of unprincipled quacks who prey upon the community. But we do claim to have made many VALUABLE DISCOVERIES in Medical Science, by which we are enabled, not only to afford temporary relief, but to effect RADICAL CURES in many cases of Chronic Disease which have been pronounced hopeless by other physicians. Devoteing, as we do, our entire attention to diseases of a chronic nature, we deem it no impudent assumption to claim GREATER SKILL than can reasonably be expected of those who divide their time between acute and chronic complaints.

We have opened a large and convenient office in South Bend, Indiana, where one of us may at any time be consulted FREE OF CHARGE by all who are suffering from any chronic complaint. For full particulars as to our principles in the treatment of disease, as well as for explicit directions to those desiring to consult us by letter, send for a copy of our paper, which will be mailed gratis to any address. Address as above.

ST. PATRICK'S SELECT SCHOOL

— FOR —

BOYS AND YOUNG MEN.

This School is Adjacent to St. Patrick's Church,

ON DIVISION, BET. SCOTT AND CHAPIN STS.

The building is 50x35 feet, with a ceiling 18 feet high, and it is divided by a folding partition into two divisions; thus making two of the most commodious study halls in the city. Both these halls may be thrown into one, when required; and as they are separated from the church by a folding partition, they may be added to it on occasions of public service or religious lectures. The windows are so adjusted as to admit the upper sash to slide downwards, thus admitting a continuous supply of fresh air, so necessary for the health and comfort of students.

The desks are constructed on an entirely new and convenient plan, projected by Father Cooney, to avoid the inconvenience and noise unavoidable with the ordinary desks, accompanied with chairs.

No chairs are used, and the seats and desks are so fixed that in a few seconds they may be changed into ordinary pews, thus making it very convenient for lectures, &c.

The school was organised by Father Cooney, in November, 1866, and consists of two departments, or divisions, according to the capacity and age of the pupils. In these departments the pupils are sub-divided into classes to suit the wants and contribute to the advancement of each scholar.

The school is under the continual supervision of the Pastor, and the classes are taught by the Brothers of the Holy Cross, who are thoroughly prepared for teaching, which their vocation requires them to make the business of their life.

All the preparatory branches, together with Book-keeping, Algebra, Geometry, and everything connected with a thorough English education, are taught in this school, thus preparing young men for any business, except the learned professions.

The school is open to all denominations. Religion is taught only to Catholic pupils. But the principles of morality are to be strictly followed by all, together with a strict adherence to propriety of language and manners, without which neither order nor discipline could be maintained in any school, and the desired advancement of the pupils would be impossible.

As *education* is the *only* object of the school, the terms are very moderate.

The scholastic year commences on the first Monday of September.

St. Mary's Academy,

NOTRE DAME, INDIANA,

Is situated on a beautiful drive, two miles from the thriving city of South Bend, and one mile from the University of Notre Dame. It is conducted by the SISTERS OF HOLY CROSS, ladies whose talent and energy, together with the cordial co-operation of the public, have secured to Indiana one of the most desirable institutions for the education of young ladies in the United States.

The Location

Is one most fortunately chosen, the rapid and health-imparting waters of the St. Joseph River, encircling the eminence on which it stands, and the wooded banks affording a pleasant theater for vigorous sports and delightful rambles.

The Grounds

Are charmingly laid out, and ornamented with summer-houses, fountains, shrines and statuary, presenting a landscape to extort the admiration of the most indifferent.

The seclusion from the town—so promotive of study—is more than compensated for, by the great attention paid to healthful amusements, which is a strong feature of the system observed at St. Mary's; indeed no expense is spared to render the young ladies cheerful and happy while pursuing their classical course.

The Buildings

Are large and well appointed, heated throughout by steam, furnished with hot and cold baths, and perfectly ventilated. They are also tastefully adorned with choice paintings, statues and oratories, the handsome Music Hall being supplied with harps, guitars, and thirty pianos, all kept in constant use.

The Laboratory

Possessess an excellent Philosophical Apparatus, and an extensive Herbarium of foreign and native plants is attached to the Botanical department.

The Plan of Teaching

With the Sisters of Holy Cross, is to *incorporate* the accomplishments upon a sound moral and scientific basis, thus to render them but the just expression of an interior culture, rather than a gilded mask to conceal a total deficiency of sound education, which we too frequently find them.

Literary and Scientific Lectures

Are afforded the pupils through the year by accomplished professors from the University of Notre Dame. Excellent facilities are also enjoyed for the study of Latin, while the modern languages receive due attention. French and German being the native tongues of several of the teachers, they are spoken in the Academy, and fluency encouraged by stated *Conversations* held in the hours of recreation.

The corps of Musical Instructors is unsurpassed, and many pupils enter for the sole object of acquiring this branch. Distinguished Professors are employed in Vocal Music, as also in the essential art of Elocution.

The Disciplinary Government

Is mild, and conducted with such energy and vigilance as always to secure perfect order and regularity. The young ladies are kept within the line of duty more by a sense of honor and justice than by fear of punishment. Pupils become the children of the House, the Sisters watching over their best interests with the solicitude of mothers.

Non-Catholic pupils are received, and are only required, for the sake of uniformity, to assist at the public and regular exercises of Religion with propriety and decorum.

A daily line of carriages is established between the Academy and the city of South Bend.

SPENCERIAN COMMERCIAL COLLEGE,

Opposite the Court House, SOUTH BEND, IND.

Student are here perfected in a thorough business education. The system pursued is of so practical a character that graduates are competent to enter at once upon the active duties of a business life. Students from abroad can be accomodated with board at reasonable rates. The country offers no better opportunity for obtaining a good business education. Professors and teachers are all competent and experienced men. Frequent lectures on commercial law and other topics.

ADAMS & SUMPTION.

RHODES & SIEGFRIED,

WHOLESALE DEALERS IN

BOOTS, SHOES, LEATHER AND FINDINGS,

A large stock of Ladies', Misses', Children's, Men's and Boy's Boots and Shoes of latest style at all times on hand and for sale at the very lowest prices. Boots and Shoes made to order. Repairing done.

Call and examine our goods and we pledge ourselves that prices and quality shall suit.

Washington, N. E. cor. Main Street, opposite Odd Fellows' Hall,
SOUTH BEND, IND.

FRIEDBERGER'S DRY GOODS AND FANCY STORE,

Washington Street, corner of Main, OPPOSITE ODD FELLOWS' HALL, SOUTH BEND, IND.

ALL KINDS OF

STAPLE AND FANCY DRY GOODS,

Of most fashionable styles, and Ladies' and Gentlemen's Furnishing Goods.

Keeps constantly on hand Hats, Caps, Zephyrs, Beltings, Nets, Buttons, Gloves, Slipper Patterns, Hosiery, Collars, Under Shirts, Drawers, Hoop Skirts, Corsets, &c. My motto is "Cheaper than the Cheapest."

M. FRIEDBERGER.

LEMEN, GRETHER & CO.,

WHOLESALE AND RETAIL DEALERS IN

BOOTS, SHOES, LEATHER & FINDINGS

All of which will be sold very low for cash. We have a complete stock of Ladies', Misses', Children's, Men's and Boy's wear of the latest and most fashionable style, and in great variety. Work made to order and warranted. Repairing done.

No. 1 Odd Fellows' Block, OPPOSITE THE COURT HOUSE. **SOUTH BEND, IND.**

Established in 1852.

Studebaker Bros.,

Manufacturers of Heavy and Light

CARRIAGES

SPRING,

FARM AND FREIGHT WAGONS,

MICHIGAN STREET,

South Bend, - - Indiana.

We invite particular attention to the superiority of our FARM WAGONS, at prices that defy competition.

Photographs of Buggies and Carriages sent to customers on application by letter. Farmers, Teamsters, Freighters and the public generally are invited to call and examine our work before purchasing.

Having had many years experience in this line of manufacture, we believe that our judgment in selecting materials, the skill of our workmen, together with the ample facilities in the way of machinery which we possess, will warrant us in representing our work equal, if not

SUPERIOR TO ANY MANUFACTURED IN THE COUNTRY,

And that we are justified in CHALLENGING COMPARISON with any and all manufactories, for excellence in material and workmanship.

ALL WORK WARRANTED.

C. Studebaker, Financial Manager. J. M. Studebaker, Gen. Manager of Manufactory. P. E. Studebaker, Salesman.

8

ANDREW ANDERSON,

ATTORNEY AT LAW,

SOUTH BEND, IND.

I HAVE IN MY OFFICE A

SET OF ABSTRACT BOOKS,

Showing all the recorded Deeds, Mortgages, Wills, Tax Sales and Judgments of or affecting the title to real estate in St. Joseph county.

I can tell the title to any farm or town lot in this county at a glance. Will furnish written and guaranteed abstracts of title on special contract, when desired.

A. ANDERSON.

J. A. CHOCKELT,

Jefferson Street, BETWEEN MICHIGAN & MAIN STS., South Bend, Ind.

MANUFACTURER OF

FARM AND SPRING WAGONS,

And all kinds of Carriages, Buggies, Sulkies, Sleighs and Bobs. Repairing done promptly and in the best manner. **HORSE SHOEING** and **BLACKSMITHING** in all its departments attended to by experienced workmen. This establishment is not as large as some others, but the quality of work cannot be excelled, and in prices we defy competition. All work warranted. Farmers and others giving us a call will see that these things are so.

NEUPERTH & BENZ,

East Side of Michigan Street, one door South of Shively's Block,

SOUTH BEND, IND.,

Have on hand a full and well selected stock of

Hardware, Cutlery, Tinware, Stoves,

And generally all articles in their line of business, which they offer at the very lowest prices which small profits and quick sales will justify. A practical knowledge of the business and strict attention to all its details will, we trust, insure perfect satisfaction. All kinds of tin work made to order, and repairing done. Our stock of stoves is very full. Give us a call and we guarantee satisfaction.

CITY HAT, CAP & FUR STORE.

WHEELER & ORVIS.

The largest and best assortment in the city. Also GENERAL SEWING MACHINE AGENTS.

No. 3 Washington Block, Sign of the Big Hat, Washington St., South Bend, Ind.

South Bend Graded School,

FOR SCHOLARS OF BOTH SEXES.

This School, so favorably known, is now open for the reception of students. The business of teaching has long been a speciality with the conductors of this school, and they are determined to continue to merit the approbation of the public. Terms adjusted on application. School Rooms in Commercial College Block, opposite the Court House, South Bend, Indiana.

☞ Mr. Sumption is Examiner of Schools of St. Joseph county.

ADAMS & SUMPTION.

KNOBLOCK BROTHERS,

MANUFACTURERS OF

IMPROVED EXTENSION TABLES,

ORDERS KINDLY SOLICITED. P. O. Box 115.

Wm. Knoblock, Theo. E. Knoblock. } **SOUTH BEND, IND.**

NOTRE DAME.
BAKER

UNIVERSITY OF NOTRE DAME.

St. Joseph County, Indiana.

THIS Institution, incorporated in 1844, enlarged in 1866, and fitted up with all modern improvements, affords accommodations to five hundred students. Situated near the M. S. & N. I. Railroad, it is of easy access from all parts of the United States. Nearly one thousand acres of land are attached to the College, all of which is well adapted both by nature and art for college purposes. The studies pursued are wide in their range, and instruction careful and thorough. A kind and parental care is exercised over all the students, and the utmost attention paid to health and morals.

TERMS:

Matriculation Fee,	$ 5 00
Board, Bed and Bedding, and Tuition,(Latin and Greek included,) washing and Mending of Linen, Doctor's Fees and Medicine and Attendance in sickness, per session of five month	152 50
French, German, Italian, Spanish and Hebrew, each	10 00
Instrumental Music	12 50
Use of Piano	10 00
Use of Violin	2 00
Drawing	10 00
Use of Philosophical and Chemical Apparatus	5 00
Graduation Fee	10 00
Students who spend their summer vacation at the College are charged extra	35 00

Payments to be made invariably in Advance.

Class Books, Stationery, &c., furnished at Current Prices.

No expenditure for Clothing nor advances for Pocket Money will be made by the Institution, unless an equivalent sum of money be deposited with the Treasurer of the College.

Each Student on entering must be provided with.

6 Shirts,	3 Pairs Boots or Shoes,
6 Pocket Handkerchiefs,	2 Suits of Clothes for Winter,
6 Pairs Stockings,	2 " " " " "
6 Towels,	1 Overcoat,
6 Napkins,	1 Table Knife, 1 Fork, 1 Tea Spoon,
1 Hat,	1 Table Spoon,
1 Cap,	Combs, Brushes, &c., for Toilet.

The first Session begins on the first Tuesday of September, the second on the first of February.

For further Particulars, address,

REV. W. CORBY, C. S. C., Pres't.

N. B. Express charges on parcels to the Students should be pre paid.

JACOB STRAYER'S PATENTS.

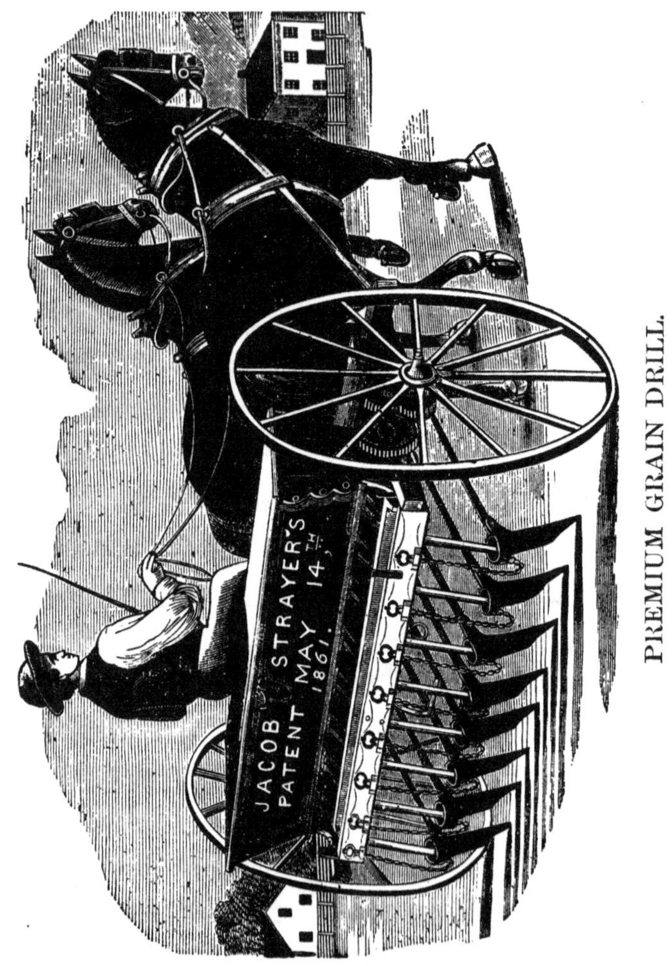

PREMIUM GRAIN DRILL.

SOUTH BEND, INDIANA.

STATESMAN

Premium Grain Drill

MANUFACTURED BY

JACOB STRAYER & CO.,

SOUTH BEND, - - - INDIANA.

We are now manufacturing the above celebrated Drill, with eight and ten hoes, double rank, with grass seed sower and surveyor, all warranted to sow wheat, rye, oats, barley, timothy and clover seed, and to be quickly regulated to sow any quantity per acre that may be desired.

This drill has taken many premiums at State and County Fairs, and what is even better, has stood the test of experience for the last seven years. It has been several times improved since the first Patent was issued, and now claims to be as near perfection as any other article of Agricultural Machinery. The Drill is

ALL THAT FARMERS CAN WISH.

Try one and you will have no reason to regret it. Drills are delivered on board the cars at South Bend, free of charge.

Those desiring Drills should apply to our Agents, or write to the Manufacturers in time. Delaying until seeding time may result in being too late for the season.

For prices see our Agents, or write to the Manufacturers.

JACOB STRAYER & CO.

SOUTH BEND

BILLIARD PARLOR

OVER KNOBLOCK & BUCHTEL'S STORE,

WASHINGTON ST.,

SOUTH BEND, IND.

We have furnished the above Parlor with FOUR of

PHELAN & CALLENDER'S TABLES,

And fitted up for the comfort and quiet of visitors.

The best of Order will at all times be observed.

LOVERS OF THE GAME ARE INVITED TO GIVE US A CALL.

S. LEWIS & SON.

STUDEBAKER BROS.,

SOUTH BEND, INDIANA,

MANUFACTURE

EVERY STYLE OF BUGGIES,

INCLUDING

LIGHT BUGGIES,

HEAVY BUGGIES,

OPEN BUGGIES,

TOP BUGGIES.

Photographs sent on application by letter. Buggies will be manufactured to order in any desirable style. We have a full force of hands specially engaged on this class of work.

Studebaker Brothers pay particular attention to all improvements in this branch of their business, and do not permit any improvements to escape their notice.

ALL WORK WARRANTED

To give full and perfect satisfaction.

Address, or call and see Studebaker Brothers, South Bend, Ind., or at ST. JOSEPH, MISSOURI.

C. STUDEBAKER. P. E. STUDEBAKER. J. M. STUDEBAKER.

D. HATCH,

In the Rear of Shively's Building,

SOUTH BEND, INDIANA,

Offers to the public generally, the advantages of

First Class Livery,

In all departments. The location is convenient, the stock and carriages of the best kind and the prices reasonable. No pains will be spared to give perfect satisfaction.

HORSES BOARDED and taken care of in the Best Manner.

Excellent accommodations and good facilities for those wishing to sell or exchange horses. Cash paid for feed and hay.

ST. JOSEPH VALLEY
BILLIARD PARLORS.

FINCH & BROTHER, Proprietors,

SOUTH BEND, IND.

This Parlor, now located in the Third Story of the Washington Building, corner of Washington and Main streets, will on the 1st of November, 1867, be removed to a spacious room, on the ground floor of the OPERA HOUSE, now building, on Washington street, opposite the Court House. We shall put in five Tables with Shulenburg & Co.'s new Patent Cushions, which are warranted to us as superior to any other Tables in the world.

The St. Joseph Valley Billiard Parlors will be conducted on strict temperance principles, and while we shall endeavor to afford first class facilities for amusement to those who love the noble game, we shall at all times, insist on the most perfect order and give no favor to rowdyism or dissipation. We invite gentlement to our Parlors and expect all who call to be such. The game of billiards disgraces no one, and no one ought to disgrace it.

A. COQUILLARD,

LIVERY AND SALE STABLES,

Corner of Washington & Jefferson Sts.,

SOUTH BEND, - - INDIANA,

Is prepared to furnish the public with Horses, Carriages, Buggies, &c., at all times and of the most superior kind and quality. I intend to give citizens and strangers perfect satisfaction.

Horses exchanged or sold to advantage, and on very reasonable terms.

CASH PAID FOR HAY, GRAIN AND FEED.

The City Supply Store of Knoblock & Buchtel can supply all articles needed in keeping house. They sell more Goods than any other Grocery House in the city. Flouring Mill and Bakery in connection.

When you start out to buy go straight to Knoblock & Buchtel's; and if you cannot go yourself, send your child with the order and they will deal fairly, and deliver the Goods without extra charge. They are also prepared to sell at Wholesale.

The above are facts, and we challenge successful contradiction.

MANY CITIZENS,

Of South Bend and St. Joseph County.

St. Joseph's Academy

SOUTH BEND, IND.

UNDER THE DIRECTION OF THE

Sisters of the Holy Cross

This Institution is beautifully situated on a most eligible, elevated and spacious lot, half way between the Court House and the depot. The building has just been finished, at a cost of nearly $20,000. The exterior elegance of the building, standing in full view at the head of Wayne street, and the rare and excellent taste with which the grounds are laid out, make it unquestionably one of the most conspicuous and attractive spots in the city.

Here, as everywhere else, after ordinary difficulties and exertions, the Sisters' School has become deservedly popular. The class of pupils thronging their halls are, of course, in keeping with their superior accommodations and the care bestowed upon them. It is unnecessary to say that the internal arrangements are all that can be desired for the comfort and advancement of young ladies at school.

A few steps from the main building, and in a separate little cottage, the Sisters have opened a minims school for young boys under ten years of age. This department is intended to supply a want much felt by parents in every city. Boys under this tender age, if they go to school at all, are thronged into schools, among boys of more advanced age, and they seldom learn much, except what is detrimental to their manners and morals. Under the mild government of the Sisters, who perform, in their regard, the duties of the best mothers, their condition is far different. This every parent will readily understand. That tender solicitude, therefore, which parents must feel for their children at that age, will doubtless bring this department a liberal patronage.

Particular attention paid to teaching the French and German languages. To accommodate a large number who desire to obtain a perfect knowledge of German, arrangements have been made for a native German teacher of elegant acquirements.

Terms are very moderate. Number of pupils attending the Academy last term, one hundred and fifty-five.

Choice White Winter Wheat Flour,
Choice Red Winter Wheat Flour,
Choice Graham Flour,
Choice Rye Flour,
Choice Buckwheat Flour,
Choice Corn Meal,
Choice Hominy,

Orders for any of the above shall receive our Best Attention. In our CUSTOM GRINDING we Warrant Entire Satisfaction.

KNOBLOCK, ZEITLER & CO.

PROPRIETORS,

ST. JOSEPH CUSTOM MILLS,

SOUTH BEND, - - INDIANA.

JOHNSTON'S NURSERY,

Devoted to the Culture of Small Fruits,

Strawberries, Raspberries, Blackberries, Grapes, &c.,

Particular attention paid to Selling Plants. New varieties always on hand.
Catalogues on application.

Washington Street, Near N. I. College, SOUTH BEND, IND.

T. G. TURNER,

Attorney & Counsellor at Law,

SOUTH BEND, INDIANA.

CHAPIN & CUSHING,

DEALERS IN

FANCY & STAPLE DRY GOODS,

Michigan Street, South Bend, Ind.

DR. W. H. HANFORD,

DENTIST,

All branches of the Business promptly attended to in the most scientific and artistic manner,

Office in Odd Fellows' Buildings,

Corner Washington and Main Steets,

SOUTH BEND, IND.

D. M. SHIVELY,

DEALER IN

STAPLE AND FANCY

DRY GOODS,

CARPETS IN GREAT VARIETY,

SHIVELY'S BLOCK,

Cor. Washington & Michigan Sts.,

SOUTH BEND, IND.

A. G. & W. F. CUSHING,

DRUGGISTS,

AND DEALERS IN

Paints, Oils, Glass, Etc.,

MICHIGAN STREET,

SOUTH BEND, INDIANA.

MISS FLORA L. TURNER,

TEACHER OF

VOCAL & INSTRUMENTAL

MUSIC,

SOUTH BEND, INDIANA.

ALEX. BERTRAND,

Bookseller, Stationer,

AND NEWS AGENT,

DEALER IN

Sheet Music and Fancy Goods,

WASHINGTON ST.,

SOUTH BEND, INDIANA.

Anderson, King & Alexander,

MANUFACTURERS OF

WHEELS & WHEEL MATERIAL

FOR WAGONS, CARRIAGES

And Agricultural Machines,

SOUTH BEND, IND.

A liberal discount on large lots and to those who buy to sell again.

J. N. CORNING,

DEALER IN

Pine, Oak and Poplar

LUMBER,

LATH,

Pine and Poplar Shingles, &c.

Cor. MAIN & DIVISION STREETS,

SOUTH BEND, IND.

VAN SICKLE'S

Fine Art Gallery

COLFAX'S STONE FRONT,

SOUTH BEND, INDIANA.

Beautiful Photographs, Ambrotypes, Porcelain and Ivorytypes in every style and variety. Photographs colored in India ink, oil or water colors.

J. B. LOTT,

Barber & Hair Dresser,

All Kinds of Perfumery for sale,

WASHINGTON ST.,

Over Knoblock's Store, South Bend, Ind.

FRANZ BAUER, JR.,

Tobacco & Cigars

Of best quality, in connection with

SALOON,

Best of Liquors and Lager Beer,

WASHINGTON ST.,

Between Main and Michigan,

SOUTH BEND, - - INDIANA.

MARTIN & SMITH,

Manufacturers of

FURNITURE,

OF ALL KINDS.

Orders will be Promptly Filled.

SOUTH BEND, IND.

JAMES BONNEY'S

PHOTOGRAPHIC

GALLERY.

Pictures Finished in

Oil, Water Colors and India Ink.

Picture Frames, &c., for Sale,

S. W. corner Washington & Michigan Sts.,

SOUTH BEND, IND.

ED. GILLEN,

DEALER IN ALL KINDS OF

Liquors, Cigars and Fruits,

FRESH OYSTERS

At Wholesale and Retail,

Washington St., bet. Main & Michigan,

SOUTH BEND, IND.

C. W. MARTIN,

MANUFACTURER OF

HARNESSES, SADDLES,

BRIDLES, &c.

WHIPS, HALTERS, TRIMMINGS

And everything in his line for sale,

East side of Michigan Street,

Bet. Washington & Market,

SOUTH BEND, IND.

JOHN H. KEEDY,

Manufacturer of Custom and Shipping

FLOUR,

Ship Stuffs, Middlings, Bran, &c.,

FOR SALE.

CASH PAID FOR WHEAT at ALL TIMES.

Office near cor. Michigan & Market Sts.,

SOUTH BEND, IND.

J. W. STOVER, M. D.,

RESIDENCE AND OFFICE:

East Side of Main, cor. Centre St.,

SOUTH BEND, IND.

C. H. MIDDLETON,

DENTIST,

Office in Colfax Block,

Michigan Street, South Bend, Ind.

DR. CHAS. H. APPLEGATE,

Office with Dr. Middleton.

L. HITCHCOCK,

DEALER IN

GROCERIES, CROCKERY

Glass Ware, Fruits, Fish, Teas,
Wood, Stone & Willow Ware,

WASHINGTON ST.,

SOUTH BEND, - - - INDIANA.

DR. J. A. BURT,

HOMŒOPATHIST,

OFFICE:

MICHIGAN ST., WEST SIDE,
Between Washington & Lafayette Sts.,

SOUTH BEND, IND.

Dr. C. F. NEVIUS,

DENTIST,

SOUTH BEND, IND.

OFFICE;

Cor. Michigan & Washington Streets.

ALL WORK WARRANTED.

DR. L. J. HAM,

OFFICE ON WASHINGTON ST.,

2d door west of Court House,

SOUTH BEND, IND.

SOUTH BEND

WOOLEN MILLS.

ALEXANDER C. STALEY.

Cash paid for Wool. Work Promptly Done.

ON THE EAST SIDE,

NEAR THE DAM.

STOCKFORD & KENT,

HOUSE, SIGN AND FANCY

PAINTING,

MAIN STREET,
First Door North of the Methodist Church,

SOUTH BEND, IND.

YOUNG & MERRIMAN,

CONFECTIONERY AND

Ice Cream Saloon,

Wholesale and Retail Dealers in

FRUITS, OYSTERS,

SEGARS & TOBACCO,

WASHINGTON STREET,
Next door east of Odd Fellows' Block,

SOUTH BEND, IND.

GEO. HAGEN,
BILLIARD SALOON
THREE FIRST CLASS TABLES,
LAGER BEER, WINE & CIGARS,
Of Best Quality.
Order and Sobriety always maintained,
MAIN STREET,
OPPOSITE ST. JOSEPH BLOCK,
SOUTH BEND, - - INDIANA.

DR. S. F. MYERS,
PHYSICIAN & SURGEON
OFFICE:
Corner Market and Michigan Streets,
Opposite the Bank,
SOUTH BEND, IND.

WILLIAM MILLER.
Keeps for sale all kinds of
LEATHER AT HIS TANNERY,
—AND—
Flour, Meal & Feed at his Mill.
Cash paid for Hides, Bark, Wheat, &c.,
AT EITHER PLACE, IN
SOUTH BEND, IND.

JOHN TREANOR,
DRUGGIST,
DEALER IN
Paints, Oils & Groceries
ALSO,
Pure Liquors and Patent Medicines
OF ALL KINDS.
WASHINGTON ST.,
SOUTH BEND, INDIANA.

A. B. CLIFFORD,
CITY BAKERY.
GROCERIES,
Confectionery, Fruits, Notions, &c.
No. 3 ST. JOSEPH BLOCK,
SOUTH BEND, IND.

JOHN GALLAGHER,
MERCHANT TAILOR
AND CLOTHIER,
WASHINGTON STREET,
SOUTH BEND, IND.

Garments cut and made to order. Furnishing Goods for sale.

ALBERT MC DONALD,
Picture Gallery,
Portrait, Landscape, Architectural
—AND—
SKY LIGHT PHOTOGRAPHS.
All kinds of Frames. Large Work a Speciality.
BARRETT'S BUILDING,
SOUTH BEND, IND.

A. B. WADE,
Attorney at Law,
SOUTH BEND, IND.

HARPER & MASSEY,

DEALERS IN

Dry Goods, Groceries,

CROCKERY, CARPETS, ETC.

Cor. Washington & Main Sts.,

SOUTH BEND, IND.

L. HUMPHREYS, M. D.,

Physician and Surgeon,

OFFICE OVER EAGLE STORE,

WASHINGTON STREET,

SOUTH BEND, - - - INDIANA.

C. G. HODSON,

CARPENTER AND BUILDER,

FOOT OF WASHINGTON ST.,

SOUTH BEND, IND.

Jobbing done at Short Notice.

GEO. A. HOWE,

DENTIST,

OFFICE ON MICHIGAN ST.,

SOUTH BEND, IND.

HUEY & CO.,

Wholesale Manufacturers of

WOOD AND CANE SEAT

CHAIRS

SOUTH BEND, IND.

J. B. ARNOLD, JR.,

Attorney at Law

AND REAL ESTATE AGENT,

Cor. Washington & Main Sts.,

SOUTH BEND, IND.

HERTZELL & HARTMAN,

MANUFACTURERS OF

Sash, Doors and Blinds.

Planing & Sawing done to order.

SOUTH BEND, IND.

GEO. HERTZELL. CHAS. HARTMAN.

CHARLES VINSON,

BUTCHER,

AND DEALER IN

Cattle, Sheep and Hogs,

WASHINGTON ST.,

Between Main and Michigan,

SOUTH BEND, INDIANA.

J. BROWNFIELD,
DEALER IN
DRY GOODS,
Groceries, Crockery, Salt,
PLASTER, WOOL, &c.
SOUTH BEND, INDIANA.

EDDY & HENDERSON,
ATTORNEYS AT LAW,
No. 5 ST. JOSEPH BLOCK,
SOUTH BEND, IND.
NORMAN EDDY. JOSEPH HENDERSON,

DUNN & CO.,
DEALERS IN
STAPLE AND FANCY
Dry Goods,
MICHIGAN STREET,
SOUTH BEND, INDIANA.
J. H. DUNN. H. G. VAN TUYL. H. S. STANFIELD.

RANDOLPH LABERDIE,
DEALER IN
Watches, Clocks
AND JEWELRY,
Also, in all kinds of
Fancy Goods & Toys,
SOUTH BEND, IND.

H. J. BLOWNEY,
DEALER IN
Paints, Oils, Varnishes,
WINDOW GLASS, ETC.,
MAIN STREET,
SOUTH BEND, INDIANA.
All kinds of Painting executed to order.

MUSSEL BROS.,
DEALERS IN
GROCERIES
CIGARS & TOBACCO,
CROCKERY & GLASS WARE,
No. 2 ST. JOSEPH BLOCK,
SOUTH BEND, IND.
G. C. MUSSEL. J. M. MUSSEL.

EDWARD BUYSSE,
DEALER IN
Watches, Clocks
AND JEWELRY,
ST. JOSEPH BLOCK,
SOUTH BEND, IND.
Repairing done in superior style and warranted.

THE NORTHWESTERN "EXCELSIOR"
MANUFACTURING COMPANY.
FULSOM, ILSLEY & CO.,
Will supply the trade with fine, coarse and medium
EXCELSIOR
For Upholstering, Mattresses, and for manufacturing Paper. Also for packing merchandise.
SOUTH BEND, IND.

F. R. TUTT. W. N. SEVERANCE.

TUTT & SEVERANCE,

ATTORNEYS AT LAW,

Claim, Real Estate & Insurance Agents,

Office No. 4 Odd Fellows' Block, Cor. Main & Washington Sts.,

SOUTH BEND, INDIANA.

W. N. SEVERANCE, NOTARY PUBLIC.

JACOB HARDMAN,

JUSTICE OF THE PEACE,

OFFICE NORTH END OF ST. JOSEPH BLOCK,

UP STAIRS,

SOUTH BEND, IND.

JAMES DAVIS,

ATTORNEY AT LAW,

OFFICE No. 8 ODD FELLOWS' BUILDING,

SOUTH BEND, INDIANA.

THOS. S. STANFIELD. ED. P. STANFIELD.

STANFIELD & STANFIELD,

ATTORNEYS AT LAW,

Old Office of Stanfield & Anderson, Lafayette Street,

SOUTH BEND, IND.

OLIVER, BISSELL & CO.,

South Bend, - - - - Indiana,

Are prepared to Manufacture all kinds of

MACHINERY CASTINGS,

PULLIES,

HANGERS,

SHAFTING, &c.

Also, Manufactured and always on hand,

Steel & Cast Iron Plows,

OF THE MOST APPROVED PATTERNS,

SINGLE & DOUBLE SHOVEL PLOWS,

SCRAPERS,

Plow Castings, Plow Points,

And generally everything in the Casting Line.

Our patterns are mostly new and of the latest styles. Patterns made for any desired castings. We pay personal attention to our business, and having had long experience, expect to be able to give the most perfect satisfaction. Call on or address

OLIVER, BISSELL & CO.

SOUTH BEND, IND.

THE GREAT

CARRIAGE & WAGON FACTORY

At South Bend, Indiana.

STUDEBAKER BROS.

The Arrangements for 1867 and 1868 are Complete.

Founded in 1852 with willing hands and stout hearts, but no capital. We have struggled upward, overcoming all discouragements, until to-day we employ

One Hundred and Thirty Hands,

And turn out MORE WORK than any other Wagon Factory in Indiana. We are willing to abide by the injunction "by their works ye shall know them." Let our works praise us; we ask no other indorsement. We claim to be

Unsurpassed in excellence of Workmanship and Material,

And we make our prices such that no prudent man will claim to undersell us. On this base we plant our flag, and here we propose to fight to the end. Confident of our ability we declare to all men that we will not surrender while a "shot remains in the locker," nor while we have the means to justify our proposed end, which we assert to be

ENTIRE AND UNCONDITIONAL SUCCESS.

Our reputation, our interests, "all we are and all hope to be," are involved in making good our pledges, and all we ask is that the public will give us a trial. If we are able, as we know we are, to maintain ourselves agains all opposition, we will vindicate our motto,

"LABOR OMNIA VINCIT."

Our stock is complete and perfect. Wagons, Carriages, Buggies, Sleighs, and all vehicles always on hand in great variety, or made to order with dispatch.

WORK FULLY WARRANTED.

STUDEBAKER BROTHERS.

THE SOUTH BEND HYDRAULIC COMPANY.

This Company has recently greatly Improved the

Race on the East Side of the St. Joseph River,

at the city of South Bend, and have put in New and Substantial Head-Gates, One Hundred feet Wide. Although the Power here is not as yet developed to its full capacity, there is sufficient now available for several large manufacturing establishments in addition to those already in operation. The location is most excellent. The lots are large, and water abundant. A portion of this Power the Company propose to Lease or Sell to persons who wish to proceed with the erection of factories.

The Company has, by purchase, the right to use and draw

One-Half of the Water of the River,

which is sufficient to supply a large number of establishments with cheap and durable power.

We extract from a recent report of R. Rose, Esq., Civil Engineer, who has made careful measurements and surveys of the capacity of the river, the following statements:

"The present stage of water, (April 19th, 1866,) gives eleven thousand one hundred and fifty-seven gross horse power, the medium stage of water gives eight thousand five hundred and one gross horse power, and low stage of water, three feet below the present water surface, gives six thousand six hundred and thirty-five gross horse power. One-half of the latter power gives to the east side of river, three thousand three hundred and seventeen and a half gross horse power.

"With the present state of development of the above power, I know of no place in the North-West which affords so favorable an opportunity for creating a great water-power, at such inconsiderable expense."

Attention is directed to the class of factories and branches of business that could be advantageously pursued here. A paper mill could not fail to be a good investment. Our proximity to the Chicago and western markets, the abundance of material, (thousands of tons of straw being annually burnt and destroyed in the county,) and the cheapness of living, are inducements that cannot be ignored.

An edge tool factory, a large woolen factory, furniture factories, wagon factories, would all find a desirable location and a good market for all their products.

We would invite the attention of capitalists, East and West, to the importance, cheapness, aud the superior advantages of this water-power.

Further information will be given upon application to the "South Bend Hydraulic Company."

Reference is made to Hon. Thomas S. Stanfield, and W. G. George, Esq., South Bend, who are well acquainted with all the advantages presented by these superior mill sites.

☞ See page 60, Turner's Gazetteer of the St. Joseph Valley.

PEAT AND FARM LANDS,

ALSO

FINE DAIRY FARMS

FOR SALE!

Lying in St. Joseph County, Indiana, 800 acres of First Quality Peat Lands; 3,600 acres of Rich Land, about 600 acres of which, is Choice Timber; 1,500 acres of Fine Prairie, and 1,500 acres Rich Bottom Lands, and can be advantageously divided into farms of from 200 to 500 acres each. The bottom land will yield annually, 3,000 tons of Hay, of good quality. The Prairie and Wood land can be used for

PASTURE AND PLOUGH LANDS,

and will furnish good rail and building timber, with shade and shelter for the stock. The whole is enclosed into eight large fields—has an abundant supply of pure water, with good building sites; and being in a healthy and well settled neighborhood, is every way adapted for the

Dairy and Stock Business.

Also about 3,000 acres of Oak, Hickory, Maple, Beach and Larch Timber Lands. The timber is of large growth and good quality.

Also,

A VALUABLE WATER PRIVILEGE

Of 150 horse power, with land sufficient for the buildings, say, from 50 to 200 acres, or more, if required. All of the above lands are well located, have a rich soil, being well watered, and are excellent for farming purposes.

The whole, or any part of the above,

WILL BE SOLD VERY LOW,

And on easy terms of Payment.

Enquire of

ISAAC ESMAY,

At the Court House, in South Bend.

MISHAWAKA, INDIANA.

The Post Office is on Vistula Street, west of Main. Col. Newton Bingham is Postmaster.

TOWN OFFICERS.

Marshal—Henry Cooper.
Clerk—Wm. H. Judkins.
Treasurer—Frank Bingham.

Trustees—1st Ward: W. Judkins.
2d Ward: Joseph Warden.
3d Ward: Joseph Whitson.
4th Ward: H. Milburn.
5th Ward: A. H. Long.
6th Ward: Henry Hane.

CHURCHES IN MISHAWAKA.

Methodist Episcopal—Corner of Vistula and Church streets. Rev. R. H. Sparks, pastor.

Presbyterian—Corner of Vistula and Mill streets. Rev. E. Scofield, pastor.

Christian Chapel—Vistula, between Mill and Spring streets. Rev. Elder Ira Chase, in charge.

Episcopal—Spring, between First and Second streets. Rev. R. Brass, pastor.

Catholic—Third, between Mill and Spring streets.

German Evangelical—Third, between Main and Mill streets. Rev. P. Wagner, pastor.

Lutheran—Front, between Main and Church streets. Rev. G. Schuster, pastor.

Evangelical Association—Barbee's Addition. Rev. Mr. Herdel, pastor.

The Masonic Organizations in Mishawaka, with their present officers, are as follows:

MISHAWAKA LODGE No. 103.

W. M.—Henry G. Niles.
S. W.—John T. Kellogg.
J. W.—Newton Bingham.
Treas.—J. H. Whitson.
Secy.—J. O. Evans.
S. D.—Thomas Pates.
J. D.—E. R. Huntsinger.
Tyler—H. H. Fraats.

MISHAWAKA COUNCIL No. 19.

T. J. M.—George Milburn, Senior.
Dept. T. J. M.—J. H. Whitson.
C. S. W.—J. T. Kellogg.
C. G.—Thomas Pates.
Recorder.—J. O. Evans.
Treasurer.—J. D. Milburn.
Sentinel.—George Hess.

ODD FELLOWS.

MONITOR LODGE No. 286.

N. G.—James Easton.
V. G.—Thomas S. Long.
Secy.—Washington Gibson.
Treas.—A. H. Long.

YOUNG MEN'S CHRISTIAN ASSOCIATION.

President—J. S. Ball.
Vice President—H. H. Judson.
" " —Mrs. Jenny Honser.
Cor. Secretary—L. F. Cole.
Rec. Secretary—Miss K. E. Merrifield.
Treasurer—Tabor Ham.
Librarian—Miss R. E. Grimes.

GEO. MILBURN & CO.,

Manufacturers of all kinds of

FARM AND SPRING

WAGONS,

Mishawaka, - - - Indiana.

Sensible of the universal tendency to anti-war prices, it has been and shall be our endeavor to touch the lowest possible point which economy in production, coupled with a perfect article, will permit. Our aim is to allow no one to surpass us in the quality of our work, and to sustain that reputation which the public have hitherto generously awarded us, as manufacturers of

MODEL WAGONS.

To this end we use none but

SELECTED AND WELL SEASONED TIMBER,

AND THE

BEST OF IRON,

And our workmen are mostly those who have for years labored with and for us to build up the large business which we now conduct. All our machinery is driven by power furnished by the beautiful

ST. JOSEPH RIVER,

The best, cheapest and most desirable motive power in the West. Whatever intelligence, industry and application can accomplish may be relied on by our correspondents and customers, as we are determined not to be surpassed in any market, either in

QUALITY OR ECONOMY OF PRICES.

We have Depositories at KANSAS CITY and NEW ORLEANS.

Address at Kansas City, MAC. B. GRAHAM.
" New Orleans, BUSBY, LITTLE & CO.

H. B. & L. W. MARTIN,

WHOLESALE MANUFACTURERS OF AND DEALERS IN

ALL KINDS OF BLACK WALNUT AND MAPLE

BEDSTEADS,

Wood and Cane Seat Chairs, Bureaus,

STANDS,

AND OTHER FURNITURE,

MISHAWAKA, IND.

Seasoned Lumber of the choicest kind only used. Immediate attention paid to filling orders.

CASH PAID FOR WALNUT, MAPLE AND POPLAR LUMBER.

BLESS, KENA & CO.,

Wholesale Manufacturers of all kinds of

FURNITURE,

INCLUDING

BEDSTEADS, BUREAUS, SOFAS, CHAIRS,

First Class Chamber Setts, Looking Glass Frames,

PILLAR EXTENSION TABLES, CENTRE TABLES, ETC.,

ALL OF THE LATEST PATTERNS,

MISHAWAKA, INDIANA.

All Furniture made from the best seasoned lumber and warranted. Cash paid for Black Walnut, Cherry, Maple and Poplar Lumber.

JUDSON, MONTGOMERY & CO.,

WHOLESALE MANUFACTURERS OF

BEDSTEADS, BUREAUS,

STANDS, CENTRE TABLES,

Plain and Fancy Pillared Extension Tables,

CHAMBER SETS,

And generally all kinds of Walnut, Oak, Cherry and Ash Household Furniture.

Mishawaka, Indiana.

ALSO,

OFFICE DESKS, BOOK CASES AND SECRETARIES,
In great variety.

We use no materials except of the very best quality and our lumber is all thoroughly seasoned.

Information given in relation to prices and any other matter connected with our business, on application by letter or otherwise.

Ours is much the

LARGEST FURNITURE MANUFACTORY IN INDIANA,

Which is a fact suggestive of our ability to do

GOOD WORK AT VERY LOW PRICES.

THE MISHAWAKA ENTERPRISE

Is published at Mishawaka, Indiana, in the Enterprise Building, Opposite Town Hall, every Saturday, at

Two Dollars Per Year in Advance.

It circulates extensively in every part of St. Joseph and adjoining counties, and is one of the best mediums of advertising in this section of the country. It aims to be a first-class paper, and its subscription list is constantly increasing.

JOB PRINTING.

In connection with the newspaper office, is a first-class

JOB PINTING OFFICE,

Lately supplied with the recent styles of type, with good presses, and conducted by competent workmen. We do not, therefore, hesitate to say that we can do all kinds of work as neatly, and as cheaply as any other office in the west.

HANDBILLS, CARDS, CIRCULARS,

BILL HEADS, BLANKS,

And generally, all kinds of printing done on short notice.

Try us once, and you will try us again.

N. V. BROWER, Proprietor.

ST. JOSEPH
IRON COMPANY,
MISHAWAKA,
ST. JOSEPH CO., - - - INDIANA.

Manufacturers of the Celebrated Mishawaka Silver Steel Hardened

PLOWS,

SHOVEL PLOWS,

CULTIVATORS, &c.

We also manufacture a large variety of Cast Iron Plows, including the Curtis Iron Beam.

Extras constantly on hand.

Castings and Machinery of all kinds made to order. We have the largest collection of patterns in Northern Indiana, and our facilities for manufacturing are unsurpassed.

The St. Joseph Iron Company's Store is at all times filled with all sorts of

DRY GOODS, GROCERIES, &C.,

Which will be sold at the lowest prices compatible with

QUICK SALES AND SMALL PROFITS.

We hold ourselves responsible for this statement:

WE WILL NOT BE UNDERSOLD!!

DODGE & MILBURN,

DEALERS IN

SHELF & HEAVY HARDWARE,

STOVES & TIN-WARE, WOODEN-WARE, DOORS, SASH,

And All Kinds of SAWS.

Mishawaka, - - - Indiana.

A. B. JUDSON & SON,

DEALERS IN

DRY GOODS, GROCERIES,

China, Glass and Queensware, Carpets, Floor and Oil Cloths,

BOOTS, SHOES, HATS, CAPS AND FURS.

Manufacturers and Dealers in READY-MADE CLOTHING.

Mishawaka, Indiana.

A. HUDSON & CO.,

BOOTS AND SHOES,

Ready-Made, and Made to Order,

IN THE BEST MANNER, AND WARRANTED,

Vistula Street, - - Mishawaka, Ind.

Joseph Heiser,

BARBER AND HAIR DRESSER,

OVER MILBURN'S STORE,

MISHAWAKA, - - - - INDIANA.

P. G. PERKINS,

MANUFACTURER OF

AXES AND EDGE TOOLS,

Especial attention given to

MILL PICKS AND SHINGLE KNIVES,

MISHAWAKA, - - - INDIANA.

A. B. JUDSON & CO.,

MISHAWAKA MILLS,

ALL WORK WARRANTED. CASH PAID FOR WHEAT.

MISHAWAKA, IND.

GEORGE H. SISSON,

ATTORNEY AT LAW, CONVEYANCER, &c.

Mishawaka, - - - Indiana.

Collections promptly attended to.

McLAFFERTY & VAN DEUSEN,

DEALERS IN

Drugs, Chemicals, Paints, Oils,

GLASS AND DYE STUFFS,

MISHAWAKA, - - - INDIANA.

MISHAWAKA WOOLEN MILLS.

PALMER & WARDEN.

MACHINERY NEW AND IN PERFECT ORDER. CASH FOR WOOL.

MISHAWAKA, IND.

Loshbough & Costello,

WHOLESALE MANUFACTURERS OF

BLACK WALNUT, POPLAR AND SCREW RAIL

BEDSTEADS, BUREAUS,

EXTENSION TABLES, WASHSTANDS, CRIBS, ETC.,

MISHAWAKA, IND.

W. J. THORNDYKE & CO.,

MANUFACTURERS OF

WHITE OAK BASKETS,

Orders Solicited and Promptly Filled. Work Warranted.

MISHAWAKA, IND.

FR. POPPENDICK,

BREWER,

SUPERIOR LAGER BEER AT WHOLESALE,

MISHAWAKA, IND.

BINGHAM & HUDSON,

DEALERS IN

Dry Goods, Groceries, Boots, Shoes

Ready-Made Clothing, Crockery, Glass Ware, &c.,

MISHAWAKA, IND.

J. H. EBERHART & CO.,

GROCERS

And Dealers in all kinds of Household Supplies,

MAIN, BELOW VISTULA STREET,

MISHAWAKA, IND.

ELIJAH TAYLOR,

Justice of the Peace, Collector & Conveyancer,

WEST SIDE—MAIN, BELOW VISTULA STREET,

MISHAWAKA, IND.

NOTTAGE & BALL,

MANUFACTURERS OF

DOUBLE STEEL AXES,

[TRUE MISHAWAKA PATTERN,]

Shingle Knives, Broad Axes, Sledges, Stone Hammers, Mill Picks, &c.

MISHAWAKA, IND.

CLARK & WHITSON,

DEALERS IN

STAPLE & FANCY DRY GOODS,

FAMILY GROCERIES,

Boots & Shoes, Crockery & Glass Ware, Hats & Caps,

READY-MADE CLOTHING AND CLOTHING MADE TO ORDER,

CORNER MAIN AND VISTULA STREETS,

MISHAWAKA, IND.

RIPPLE MILLS.

A. CASS & CO.

Custom Work promptly done and Warranted. Highest Market Price for Wheat.

Foot of Main Street, Mishawaka, Ind.

EXCHANGE, BANKING AND COLLECTION HOUSE.

A. B. JUDSON & SON,

MISHAWAKA, IND.

T. S. COWLES,

Attorney at Law, Notary Public,

COLLECTOR AND CONVEYANCER,

MISHAWAKA, IND.

WAGONS!

Farm Wagons, Spring Wagons.

GEORGE MILBURN & CO.,

PROPRIETORS OF THE GREAT WATER-POWER

Wagon Manufactory,

AT MISAWAKA, IND.,

Offer at greatly REDUCED PRICES, at wholesale or retail, a great variety of their celebrated Wagons, all of which, in every particular, are FULLY WARRANTED. The system to which we have reduced our business, the superior quality of the material at our command, the excellence of the mechanical ability in our employment, together with a long experience are grounds for the assurance that

The Quality of our Work shall not be Surpassed,

And that while realizing a reasonable profit, we WILL NOT BE UNDERSOLD. We have studied the requirements of the public and are determined to meet all demands.

We have always on hand at our depositories at Mishawaka, Kansas City and New Orleans, great numbers and all varieties of Wagons, which buyers are invited to examine.

Address George Milburn & Co., Mishawaka, Ind.
" Mac B. Graham, Kansas City, Mo.
" Busby, Little & Co., New Orleans, La.

ELKHART, INDIANA.

R. K. Brush is Postmaster at Elkhart. A new Post Office is soon to be built, almost exactly like the one at South Bend.

TOWN OFFICERS.

Marshal—Geo. M. Colburn.
Clerk—S. E. Smith.
Treasurer—S. Maxon.
Assessor—Albert Burns.
Attorney—Hon. M. F. Shuey.
Trustees—A. M. Tucker.
C. Beardsley.
C. J. Gillett.

CHURCHES IN ELKHART.

Episcopal—Conley's Hall. Rev. Mr. Averill, pastor.
Baptist—Pigeon street. Rev. Mr. Russell, pastor.
Presbyterian—Corner High and Second streets. Rev. J. W. Fowler, pastor.
Methodist—Second, between High and Franklin streets. Rev. Mr. Lacey, pastor.
Lutheran—Conley's Hall. Rev. R. F. Delo, pastor.
Spiritualists—City Hall.
German Methodist.

MASONIC ORGANIZATIONS.

KANE LODGE No. 183.

W. M.—O. H. Main.
S. W.—J. R. Tallerday.
J. W.—Lan. C. Patrick.
Treas.—Jac. Arisman.
Secy.—B. Tumock.

EAGLE LODGE, U. D.

W. M.—Uri Case.
S. W.—Dr. C. S. Frink.
J. W.—Milton Miller.
Secy.—A. M. Tucker.
Treas.—C. North.

ODD FELLOWS.

N. G.—Jesse Rnsh.
V. G.—C. H. Chase.
Perm't Secy.—M. Truby.
Term Secy.—J. Boster.
Treas.—H. Neal.

R. STODDARD GEE. CHAS. W. GEE.

R. STODDARD GEE & SON,

Dealers in

PIANO FORTES,

Cabinet Organs, Melodeons, Violins, Guitars, Flutes,

ACCORDEONS, SHEET MUSIC,

And All Kinds of MUSICAL INSTRUMENTS.

ALSO,

CLOAK AND DRESS MAKING,

MILLINERY AND FANCY GOODS.

Agricultural Block, Corner of Main and High Streets. Four doors south of Conley's Hall.

P. O. Box 517. **ELKHART, IND.**

R. STODDARD GEE & SON,

Having located in this place for the purpose of carrying on a general music business, offer rare inducements to those who may favor us with their patronage. We offer to the lovers of music the celebrated MATT PIANO, which, with its modern (patented) improvements, the beauty and style of workmanship, the smoothness and uniformity of tone; the blending of sounds, the advantages derived from the *Dialutic Sounding Board*, all combine to make them a superior instrument, to any other ever offered to the public, for the *same amount of money*.

Being in connection with L. J. Hoeffner, Esq., so long and favorably known as a *Piano tuner and repairer*, we keep all pianos we sell in perfect tune, for one year, *free of charge*.

We buy for CASH, and are the only agents in Ohio or Indiana who can buy these instruments direct from the factory, (all reports to the contrary being incorrect), giving us facilities for offering a better piano, and for less money, than any other agent.

SECOND-HAND PIANOS and Melodeons taken in part payment for new instruments.

PIANOS TO RENT, and if purchased in four months, the rent to apply on the purchase.

MELODEONS TO RENT.

Millinery, Dress and Cloak Making done with neatness and dispatch by workmen from Chicago.

MABLEY & BROTHER,

DEALERS IN

READY-MADE

CLOTHING,

OF ALL QUALITIES, STYLES AND PRICES,

HATS, CAPS, AND GENTLEMEN'S FURNISHING GOODS

Of all kinds. We have also, always on hand, a large stock of

Cloths, Cassimeres, Vestings, &c.,

Of the most Fashionable Styles and suited to the season, which will be made to Order, in a Superior Manner and warranted to fit. We have come to Elkhart to stay; and, if First-Class Goods, Low Prices, and Fair Dealing are desirable, we expect to make our business mutually beneficial to ourselves and the public. Give us a call and see. Remember,

"THE NEW YORK CLOTHING STORE,"

ELKHART, IND.

C. B. MANN & CO.,

Dealers in

STAPLE & FANCY DRY GOODS,

GROCERIES, ETC.,

ELKHART, IND.

Cloths, Cassimeres, Vestings, Silks; all kinds of Ladies' Dress Goods, Hoops, Skirts, Muslins, Sheetings, and generally, a Full Assortment of the

MOST FASHIONABLE GOODS,

Selected with great care, and to be sold at

VERY LOW PRICES.

Indeed, our determination is to

GIVE PERFECT SATISFACTION AND NEVER BE UNDERSOLD.

RAYMOND & KIBBE,

DRUGGISTS,

AND DEALERS IN

Paints, Oils, Glass, Confectionery, Perfumery,

GROCERIES, PURE LIQUORS, ETC.

ELKHART, IND.

C. BEARDSLEY,

MANUFACTURER OF AND DEALER IN

PRINTING & WRAPPING PAPER

All Orders promptly attended to. Cash paid for rags.

ELKHART, IND.

S. M. CUMMINS,

DENTIST,

Office over Bucklen's Drug Store, Opposite Clifton House,

ELKHART, IND.

DR. D. H. RUNYAN,

HOMŒOPATHIC PHYSICIAN,

OFFICE: MAIN STREET, Opposite Bank,

ELKHART, IND.

O. H. MAIN,

Attorney at Law, Notary Public,

GENERAL CONVEYANCER, ETC.,

Licensed to practice in all the Courts of the State,

ELKHART, IND.

CLIFTON HOUSE.

B. F. BROWN, Proprietor,

FIRST CLASS HOTEL IN EVERY RESPECT.

Elkhart, Ind.

A. E. FABER,

SALOON, RESTAURANT and BILLIARDS,

MAIN STREET, Seven Doors South of Clifton House,

ELKHART, IND.

ISAAC BUCKLEN,

DEALER IN

Drugs and Medicines, Paints, Oils, Glass,

DYE STUFFS, ETC., ETC.,

ELKHART, IND.

☞ Physicians' Prescriptions Carefully Prepared. ☜

ELKHART MARBLE WORKS

D. M. & N. P. DOTY,

MANUFACTURERS AND DEALERS IN

Tombstones, Monuments and Building Stone,

ELKHART, IND.

JOHN T. LANMAN,

DRUGGIST,

AND DEALER IN ALL KINDS OF

Medicines, Paints, Oils, Glass, Dye Stuffs, Confectionery, &c.,

ELKHART, IND.

Railroad Eating House & Hotel.

PATRICK & SON, Proprietors,

ELKHART, IND.

☞ ALL TRAINS STOP HERE FOR MEALS.

GOSHEN, INDIANA.

William L. Bivins is Postmaster at Goshen.

ELKHART COUNTY OFFICERS.

Auditor—E. W. H. Ellis.
Treasurer—Wm. H. Venamon.
Clerk—E. J. Wood.
Recorder—B. C. Dodge.
Sheriff—E. R. Kerstetter.
Commissioners—Nathaniel Thompson.
John E. Thompson.
Jacob Bechtel.

CORPORATION OFFICERS.

Trustees—Allen Smith, Wm. A. Barnes, Charles F. Butterfield, Daniel Haberstich, A. H. Blake.

Clerk—E. G. Chamberlain.
Treasurer—Joseph Lauferty.
Assessor—Moses Simmons.
Marshal—Samuel Trump.

CHURCHES IN GOSHEN.

Methodist—Main street. Rev. Geo. Newton, pastor.
Presbyterian—Market street. Rev. H. L. Van Nuys, pastor.
Baptist—Washington street. Rev. A. M. Buck, pastor.
Lutheran—Fifth street. Rev. John Weaver, pastor.
German Methodist—Fifth street.
Catholic—Madison street. Rev. M. Stores.
Episcopal—Market street.

The Masonic Organizations in Goshen are as follows:

GOSHEN LODGE No. 12.

W. M.—George W. Gibbon.
S. W.—Milo S. Hascall.
J. W.—Charles Perkins.
Treas.—C. F. Butterfield.
Secy.—E. G. Chamberlain.

FRAVEL LODGE No. 306.

W. M.—Henry Miltenberger.
S. W.—Henry Warren.
J. W.—A. H. Elwood.
Treas.—W. H. Thomas.
Secy.—H. J. Bierly.

GOSHEN CHAPTER No. 45.

High Priest.—John Ginter.
King.—Chas. F. Butterfield.
Scribe.—David Darr.
Capt. of H.—C. E. Lawrence.
P. S.—E. J. Wood.
Treas.—James Lauferty.
Secy.—E. G. Chamberlain.

ODD FELLOWS' ORGANIZATION.

ELKHART COUNTY LODGE No. 34.

N. G.—D. M. Clymer.
V. G.—John Scroggs.
Perm't. Secy.—Daniel Fravel.
Rec. Sec.—Ira Nash.
Treas.—John S. Freeman.

ENCAMPMENT No. 7.

Ch. Patriarch.—John S. Freeman.
High Priest.—D. M. Clymer.
Senr. Warden.—Hezekiah Crowell.
Secy.—J. D. Arnold.
Treas.—Wm. L. Bivans.

Established in 1837.

The Oldest Paper in Northern Indiana.

The Goshen Democrat

IS PUBLISHED AT

GOSHEN, INDIANA,

Every Wednesday morning. It has the LARGEST CIRCULATION of any paper in the county of Elkhart, and affords superior advantages to advertisers. Terms for advertising reasonable. Terms of subscription, $2.50 per annum, invariably in advance.

JOB PRINTING,

Of all kinds neatly and promptly done. Address

HERB. S. FASSETT, Publisher.

Bristol Steam Flouring Mills

With Four Runs of Stones, Engine, Boiler and Machinery,

ALL COMPLETE,

FOR SALE CHEAP.

One-fourth cash, balance in three annual instalments. Address

E. W. H. ELLIS, Goshen, Ind.

M. B. HASCALL. C. B. ALDERMAN.

HASCALL & ALDERMAN,

DEALERS IN

Staple and Fancy Dry Goods, Groceries,

BOOTS & SHOES, HATS & CAPS, CROCKERY, CARPETS, &c.,

At the Old Stand, corner Main & Market Sts., GOSHEN, IND.

L. A. MARSHALL & CO.,

WHOLESALE DEALERS IN

Foreign and Domestic Wines, Liquors & Cigars,

And Manufacturers of Caldwell's Herb Bitters,

Main Street, GOSHEN, IND.

GREAT

Hydraulic Power

—AT—

GOSHEN, INDIANA!

The water-power at this point is created by damming the Elkhart river, one mile south of the corporate limits of the town, and conveying the water by a

CAPACIOUS CANAL,

One Hundred feet in width, to the heart of the town, where it is emptied into the original channel,

WITH A FALL OF TWENTY FEET,

Furnishing power equal to one hundred and fifty run of stones. The location for mills and manufactories, for the extent of half a mile along the canal, are unsurpassed for convenience and safety. The work will be completed early in the spring of 1868, at a total cost of nearly one hundred thousand dollars, and meanwhile, the public are invited to examine the locations and facilities for business.

Goshen, the County Seat of Elkhart County, is situated near its geographical center, at the foot of Elkhart prairie, on the air line of the Michigan Southern railroad, and is surrounded by an agricultnral region of unrivaled wealth and fertility. Its present population is 3,200, and it is rapidly increasing in wealth and numbers. On the west side of town commences the great timber region, comprising more than one hundred square miles of choice timber, such as Black Walnut, Poplar, Oak, Cherry, Basswood, Elm, Ash and Hickory. More than one million feet of Walnut lumber is shipped from the station annually.

Provision is already made for the erection of two large flouring mills, a furniture manufactory and wagon shop, and the location offers great inducements for the establisment of other manufactories, such as a paper mill, woolen manufactory, carding machines, an oil mill, a chair factory, iron foundries, cotton and flax mills, and various other manufactories of wood an iron.

The company own extensive

Grounds which will be Sold or Leased with the Power.

The water will be placed at a very low rental during the first season.

The officers of the Company are Milton Mercer, President; E. W. H. Ellis, Secretary and Treasurer; Adam Yeakel, M. M. Latta, Cephas Hawks, and John Stauff, Directors; any one of whom may be addressed on the subject.

Goshen, Indiana, August, 1867.

BRISTOL
HYDRAULIC COMPANY,
Bristol, Elkhart County, Indiana.

CAPITAL STOCK, - - - - $50,000.

President, Wm. Palin; Treasurer, Wm. Caldwell; Secretary, Chas. W. Wilcox; Directors, Wm. Palin, Wm. Caldwell, Solomon Fowler, Wm. J. Hall, Simon Pickel.

This Company was organized July 17, 1867, for the purpose of improving the water-power on the St. Joseph river, at Bristol, for manufacturing purposes. The head-race of this improvement will be 1,900 feet long, on each side of which will be convenient tail races, fifty feet wide on the bottom, and nearly as low as the bed of the river. The river, at the place selected for a dam, is about two hundred and fifty feet in width at the surface, and averaging eight feet in depth. Between the head and tail races are building lots, varying from fifty to one hundred feet front, and from seventy-five to one hundred and fifty feet in depth. The great head race is one hundred and fifty feet wide on the bottom, with five feet in depth of water. The head gates have a clear water way of six hundred square feet. There will be an available fall of about six feet, with ample grounds for the proper display of the power. There is a front on the main race of nearly two thousand six hundred lineal feet. There will be ample preparation made for the lockage and passage of steamboats through the main race.

The head race, which at the top water line will be one hundred and seventy feet wide, together with a road way on each side thereof, of thirty-five feet in width, will make a clear space of two hundred and forty feet between the manufacturing establishments when erected, thus securing all from the usual risk from fire. The dam is to be three hundred feet long, and the abutments to the same and the head gates, will be of massive stone masonry, and well laid in hydraulic lime.

The entire cost of the work when completed, will not fall short of forty-five thousand dollars. At the present stage of the river, which is its minimum, the discharge of water is not less than two hundred thousand cubic feet per minute, which will give to the Company, upon wheels properly constructed, a power more than sufficient to drive three hundred mill stones as usually estimated. Three years out of five, the river discharges a much greater quantity of water per minute than is stated above. This fact shows the actual power to be much greater than the estimate given, but it is thought to be safest to take the minimum discharge as the basis.

If the Company should hereafter desire to increase their power to double that which they now have, it can be done at a comparatively small cost—probably for one-third the sum now estimated. Everything will be so constructed as to require, hereafter, no alteration or addition, should it be necessary to bring into requisition more power by adding to the work already done.

The entire work will be completed in a few months, all, probably, with the exception of the dam, before the first of December, 1867. The Company will guarantee to have the power ready for use as soon as persons desiring water power, can have their estsblishments ready for the water. Plats of the entire work, will be ready for distribution in a short time, and those desiring a location for any manufacturing purpose, can be accommodated with a lot eligibly situated, with water power, on fair terms.

This great hydraulic improvement is located on the line of the M. S. & N. I. railroads, nearly midway between Toledo and Chicago. The site is beautiful, safe, and easily improved. It is in the midst of a healthy and fine agricultural region, possessing all the advantages of a large town, good markets, and cheap living. Address the President, Secretary, or any of the Directors, or call on them, at Bristol, Elkhart County, Indiana.

SAMUEL B. ROMAINE,
Broker, Claim & Insurance Agent
PRODUCE AND LUMBER DEALER,
BRISTOL, IND.

SOLOMON FOWLER,
DEALER IN PRODUCE,
CASH PAID FOR WHEAT AND CORN,
BRISTOL, IND.

WM. C. BIRCH. ANDREW AITKEN.
BIRCH & AITKEN,
DEALERS IN
DRY GOODS, GROCERIES, CROCKERY,
Hardware, Notions, Boots, Shoes, Hats, Caps, &c.,
BRISTOL, IND.
☞ **Highest Price Paid for Country Produce.** ☜

W. PROBASCO,
DEALER IN
DRY GOODS, GROCERIES, HARDWARE,
CROCKERY, BOOTS, SHOES, HATS, CAPS,
AND IN ALL KINDS OF COUNTRY PRODUCE,
Bristol, Indiana.

BRISTOL HOUSE, FORMERLY ADAMS HOUSE, **BRISTOL, IND.**
F. M. ROE, Proprietor,
FREE OMNIBUS TO AND FROM TRAINS.
LIVERY ESTABLISHMENT CONNECTED WITH THE HOUSE.

THE REPUBLICAN,

A QUARTO WEEKLY NEWSPAPER,

IS PUBLISHED EVERY SATURDAY MORNING, AT THE

CITY OF COLDWATER, MICHIGAN,

—BY—

W. J. & O. A. BOWEN,

AT TWO DOLLARS A YEAR IN ADVANCE.

It will advocate Republican principles, and in connection therewith, discuss the polity and principles of our government.

The family circle will be well supplied with the choicest and most readable matter.

The paper will contain the latest and best acts and results in science, art, natural history and agriculture.

Our quarto form we think cannot fail to please.

We shall endeavor to so arrange and limit the quality of advertising matter as to best serve the interests of advertising patrons, and to avoid every occasion of charging us with parsimony.

GEO. A. COE,

Attorney at Law, Justice of the Peace,

And U. S. Court Commissioner,

OFFICE IN MICHIGAN SOUTHERN HOTEL BUILDING,

COLDWATER, MICH.

E. G. PARSONS,

Attorney at Law and Solicitor in Chancery,

OFFICE IN THE MASONIC BLOCK,

COLDWATER, MICH.

W. J. BOWEN,

Attorney at Law & Circuit Court Commissioner,

COLDWATER, MICHIGAN.

SOUTHERN MICHIGAN HOTEL,

North-west corner of Public Square,

COLDWATER, MICH.,

M. L. STRONG, Proprietor.

SPAULDING, DIBBLE & CO.,

DEALERS IN

STAPLE & FANCY DRY GOODS

41 Chicago Street, Coldwater, Mich.

☞ The only exclusively Dry Goods House in the city.

EXCELSIOR DINING HALL,

S. N. CORNELL, PROPRIETOR,

MONROE STREET, COLDWATER, MICHIGAN.

Warm Meals prepared at all Hours.

J. W. SHIVELY,

WHOLESALE AND RETAIL DEALER IN ALL KINDS OF

DRY GOODS & DRY GROCERIES,

COLDWATER, MICHIGAN.

LOUIS T. N. WILSON,

Attorney & Counsellor at Law,

COLDWATER, MICH.

HAMLET B. ADAMS,

Attorney at Law & Solicitor in Chancery,

COLDWATER, MICH.

WATER CURE INFIRMARY,

IN

COLDWATER, MICH.

ON THE MICHIGAN SOUTHERN AND NORTHERN INDIANA R. R.

The Building is new, built expressly for the business, and is permanently located.

To the Diseased,—those who are sick and considered incurable,—who are suffering with pain and can find no relief,—who are paralyzed and have been given up by physicians,—who are near dying—we bid you hope—your health may yet be restored.

The following diseases are positively and permanently cured by

ELECTROPATHIC TREATMENT,

without pain or inconvenience:

Palsy, or Paralysis of every variety; Consumption, Rheumatism, Acute and Chronic Neuralgia; Torpid Liver; Bronchitis, Catarrh, Asthma, Spinal Complaints, Scrofula, Dyspepsia, Deafness of all kinds, Blindness and Weak Eyes, St. Vitus Dance, Salt Rheum, Prolapsus Uteri, Piles, Female Weakness and Irregularities, General Debilty, Stiff Joints, Constipation and every specie of Chronic and Nervous diseases.

We treat the above diseases with great success if they are curable. We make no compromise with the stomach in the way of drugs. We claim to be purely Eclectic, relying much upon Water and Electricity.

Electricity is the natural element of the nervous system—the connecting link between mind and matter, the most absolute and subtle substance known. It circulates the blood; is the cause of voluntary and involuntary motion; produces all the chemical changes in the system--decompositions and recompositions, and always co-operates with vitality in imparting health and strength to the human system. If Electricity is the generating agent of human life, how important it must be in the continuance of that life, and in the preservation of health!

Electricians have for ages witnessed the astonishing effects of Electricity from their own random experiments, in controlling the most obstinate diseases, and have attributed their frequent failures more to their own ignorance than to any lack of virtue in the agent; and it has for a long time been the opinions of the most scientific investigators, that it was the vitalizing, animating, sustaining, and all-controlling power, which, if properly applied to the human system, would regulate and control all the various functions of life.

Mrs. Jane R. Willson, M. D., a lady of much experience, is with me, to take charge of the female department.

For further particulars, address

H. F. BROWN, M. D., Proprietor.

P. O. Box, 130. **COLDWATER, MICH.**

O. B. QUIGLEY,

Livery & Sale Stable,

COLDWATER, MICHIGAN.

The best of Horses, the best of Carriages, the best of everything in the Livery line.

Horses Sold or Exchanged on Fair Terms.

The best of Hacks in the city running to and from the cars, and any part of the city.

Stages for Marshall, Union City, and Angola.

CASH FOR HAY AND ALL KINDS OF GRAIN AND FEED.

THE

COLDWATER SENTINEL

IS PUBLISHED EVERY FRIDAY, AT THE CITY OF

COLDWATER, MICHIGAN,

BY SMITH & MOORE, AT

TWO DOLLARS PER ANNUM, IN ADVANCE.

It has a large circulation, and is an excellent medium for advertising.

THE ADVERTISING RATES ARE AS FOLLOWS:

One square, (ten lines), one to three weeks,	$1.00.
" " three months,	2.50.
" " six months,	4.00.
" " twelve months,	7.00.
One quarter column, one year,	25.00.
One-half column, one year,	40.00.
One column, one year,	75.00.

ST. JOSEPH'S ACADEMY,

SOUTH BEND, IND.

UNDER THE DIRECTION OF THE

SISTERS OF HOLY CROSS.

No resident of this thriving young city need be told of the beauty and healthfulness of the site of this institution. It is situated on Gen. Taylor street, at the head of Wayne, on, perhaps, the highest spot of ground in the city, of which, it commands a full view. The grounds of the academy are well laid out, and embrace a full acre, reaching from Gen Taylor street to Scott, thus affording ample space to the pupils for recreation.

The building has been finished at an expense of nearly twenty thousand dollars, and has everything that could be desired, or the dictate of *experience* could reasonably require for an educational establishment.

The building being extensive, the pupils have the invaluable advantage of well ventilated halls for preparing their classes, separate from their recitation rooms. And, exteriorly, the building is an ornament of the city, so beautiful in itself!

The Sisters, as teachers, need no eulogy; for even those who have not known them by experience, could not have failed to know them through others, since their praise as efficient teachers of manners, morals, and science combined, is upon the lips of the many who can speak of them from experience.

The regular course of studies in this institution, embraces all the branches required to complete a thorough education, including Music, vocal and instrumental, Drawing and Painting; the various branches of Needle Work; the French, German and Latin languages.

To meet the wishes of German parents, and others who may desire a thorough course in the German language, a department exclusively German, has been opened in the academy, which is under the charge of native, German Sisters. Thus affording more than ordinary facility in the acquisition of a language, after the English, the most useful to the inhabitants of the Western States.

A few steps from the academy, the Sisters have opened a "Minim School" for boys under ten years of age. This department is intended to supply a want much felt by parents in every city. Boys under this tender age, if they go to school, at all, are crowded into schools among associates of a more advanced age, and they seldom learn much except what is detrimental to their manners and morals. Under the mild government of the Sisters, who perform, in their regard, the duties of the best of mothers, their condition is far different. This every parent will readily understand. That tender solicitude, therefore, which parents must feel for their children at that age, will, doubtless, bring this department a liberal patronage.

From the above it may be seen, that the educational wants of the citizens of South Bend, are, in this institution, fully supplied; and their liberal patronage hitherto, shows that they appreciate the advantages thus placed within their reach. Terms are very moderate.

THE

MICHIGAN SOUTHERN

RAILROAD

With its connections, the MOST RELIABLE ROUTE to all points in the Eastern States and the Dominion of Canada.

Four Express Trains leave Chicago daily

CONNECTIONS ARE

At **DETROIT** with Grand Trunk and Great Western Railways.
At **TOLEDO** with Lake Shore and Dayton & Michigan Railroads.
At **CLYDE** and **MONROEVILLE** with Trains for all points in Central and Southern Ohio.
At **CLEVELAND** with Atlantic & Great Western, Cleveland & Pittsburg.
At **DUNKIRK** with Erie Railway.
At **BUFFALO** with Erie, and New York Central Railways, for all points in New York and the New England States.

Passengers coming West by the South Shore Line have choice of Four Express Trains from *Toledo* over this first-class Road.
Or, coming to DETROIT via the Canada Roads,
then connect with the MICHIGAN
SOUTHERN, through from

DETROIT TO CHICAGO WITHOUT CHANGE

Elegant and most comfortable Sleeping Cars are run on all Night Trains. Through to DETROIT and CLEVELAND without change.

Salisbury's Patent Dusters are used on Day Trains, and, also, the most comfortable and well ventilated Smoking Cars in the country.

We hold out the following inducements for public patronage:

GOOD, CLEAN EATING HOUSES.

Luxurious Sleeping Cars---Day Coaches with all Modern Improvements.

A SMOOTH TRACK,

Not second to any on this Continent. And,

FARE ALWAYS AS LOW AS BY COMPETING LINES.

The new and elegant Passenger Depot at Chicago, erected this season, is a great object of interest.

Tickets by this popular route may be had at all principal ticket offices in the United States.

C. F. HATCH, **Gen. Supt.,** Chicago, Ill.

SAML. C. HOUGH, **Gen. Pass'r Agt.,** Chicago, Ill.

NICAR, DEMING & CO.,

Wholesale and Retail Dealers in all kinds of

HARDWARE, STOVES

AND TINWARE,

Cor. Washington and Michigan Sts.,

SOUTH BEND, IND.

Always on hand and for sale at the very lowest figure,

Iron, Steel, Nails, Glass, Putty, Paints, Oils, Brushes,

AND ALL KINDS OF BUILDING HARDWARE.

ALSO,

AGRICULTURAL IMPLEMENTS,

COOPER'S AND CARPENTER'S TOOLS,

Leather and Rubber Belting,

Circular, Mill and Cross Cut Saws,

ROPES AND CORDAGE,

CUTLERY, GLUE, ETC., ETC,

All kinds of Tin Work Made to Order.

AGENTS FOR

The "La Belle" Nail Works, Wheeling, West Virginia; Laffel & Baldwin's Union Churns; William Mann & Co.'s Mishawaka Pattern Axes. Also, Genuine Mishawaka Axes.

DWIGHT HOUSE,

SOUTH BEND, INDIANA,

A. A. ALLEN, Proprietor,

Formerly of the Bramble House, Lafayette, Indiana,

I have leased the Dwight House for a term of years, and after October 1, 1867, shall be glad to see all my old friends and the public generally there. See page 99 of this Gazetteer.

A. A. ALLEN.

WM. KNOBLOCK. THEO. E. KNOBLOCK.

KNOBLOCK BROTHERS,

MANUFACTURERS OF

IMPROVED

Extension Tables,

ORDERS KINDLY SOLICITED.

Post Office Box 115.

SOUTH BEND, IND.

J. C. & C. W. HORR,

MANUFACTURERS OF

FACTORY CHEESE,

AND WHOLESALE DEALERS IN

FACTORY, CHEDDER, ENGLISH DAIRY,

Hamburg and Western Reserve Cheese,

WELLINGTON, Lorain County, OHIO.

☞ All orders promptly filled at the lowest market prices.

E. M. PLIMPTON,

Attorney and Counsellor at Law,

AND SOLICITER IN CHANCERY,

BUCHANAN, BERRIEN COUNTY, MICHIGAN.

HENRY A. FORD,

Attorney & Counsellor at Law,

AND SOLICITOR IN CHANCERY,

NILES, MICH.

Soldiers' Claims adjusted; Back Pay, Bounty and Pensions obtained. Collections promptly made.

EDSON FOSTER,

DEALERS IN

DRY GOODS, GROCERIES,

Glass and Earthen Ware, Boots, Shoes, Hats, Caps,

PLOWS, FARMERS' TOOLS, &c.,

MIDDLEBURY, - - - Elkhart County, - - - INDIANA.

CASH FOR PRODUCE.

NEW PAPER!

THE LYCEUM BANNER,

PUBLISHED TWICE A MONTH, BY

MRS. L. H. KIMBALL,

—AT—

167 SOUTH CLARK STREET, CHICAGO, ILL.

EDITED BY MRS. H. F. M. BROWN.

It is an OCTAVO, printed on good paper and embellished with fine electrotype illustrations.

Some of our best writers are engaged as regular contributors.

We teach no human creeds; Nature is our Law-giver; to deal justly our religion.

The children want Amusement, History, Romance, Music; they want Moral, Mental and Physical culture. We hope to aid them in their search for these treasures.

TERMS OF SUBSCRIPTION:

One year, ONE DOLLAR, in advance.

10	copies,	to one address	$ 9.00
25	do.	do.	22.00
50	do.	do.	45.00
100	do.	do.	90.00

Subscribers in Canada must pay twenty cents per year in addition, for prepayment of American postage.

Subscribers wishing the direction of their paper changed must always state the name of the town, county and State to which it has been sent.

Money can be sent by Postoffice Orders, but when drafts on New York or Boston can be procured, we prefer them.

All subscriptions discontinued at the expiration of the time subscribed for.

☞ Specimen copies, Five cents.

All communications should be addressed to

MRS. LOU. H. KIMBALL,
P. O. Drawer 5956, CHICAGO, ILL.

DEMOCRATIC UNION,

A FIRST CLASS WEEKLY NEWSPAPER,

PUBLISHED AT

White Pigeon, ST. JOSEPH COUNTY, **Michigan,**

—BY—

GEORGE C. HACKSTAFF.

The Union affords an excellent medium for advertising, and aims to be a good Family Newspaper.

JOB PRINTING,

Of all kinds neatly and promptly done at reasonable prices.

MOWBRAY & BUCKLEY,

No. 4 ST. JOSEPH BLOCK,

SOUTH BEND, - - - - INDIANA,

DEALERS IN ALL KINDS OF

Confectionery, Canned Fruits, Nuts

PICKLES, SAUCES, CIGARS, ETC.

LADIES' & GENTLEMEN'S RESTAURANT.

WARM MEALS OF CHOICEST AND BEST KINDS,
Served at all hours.

DAY BOARDERS ACCOMMODATED.

GREEN FRUIT IN THEIR SEASON.

NO LIQUORS SOLD.

BERRIEN COUNTY ABSTRACT OFFICE.

BACON & KING,

Real Estate Agents,

NILES, MICHIGAN.

Particular attention paid to the making of Abstracts of Titles in Berrien county, to the payment of Taxes, perfecting titles, and the foreclosure and collection of mortgages. Collections will be promptly attended to.

D. BACON, Attorney at Law. JOHN KING.

H. S. TOWLE,

ATTORNEY AT LAW,

(With Goodwin & Larned,)

McCormick's Building, P. O. Box 384. CHICAGO, ILL.

FULSOM, ILSLEY & CO.,

Have dissolved by mutual consent and the business of the

North-western "Excelsior" Manufacturing Co.

Will hereafter be carried on by

FULSOM & GRANNIS.

See page 123, this Gazetteer.

A. V. P. DAY,

DEALER IN

BOOTS & SHOES,

ADRIAN, MICH.

BOND & CHANDLER,

Engravers on Wood and Label Printers,

COLORED LABELS OF ALL KINDS MADE TO ORDER,

(SMITH & NIXON'S BUILDING,)

S. W. Cor. Washington & Clark Sts., **CHICAGO, ILL.**

THREE RIVERS MILLS,

THREE RIVERS, ST. JOSEPH COUNTY, MICH.

HAMILTON & RUCKMAN,

PROPRIETORS.

We manufacture Flour from best selected White and Amber Wheat, and warrant our productions strictly first class Family Flour. Our mill has recently been put in excellent repair, and we are now using six runs of stones constantly. Our power is abundant and constant, not being materially affected by drouths or freshets. Cars on the St. Joseph Valley Railroad deliver wheat and take flour from our mill without expense of drayage.

☞ Ship Stuff in small or large quantities always for sale.

HAMILTON & RUCKMAN.

SOUTH BEND NURSERIES.

SMALL FRUITS CULTIVATED IN PERFECTION.

Strawberries, Raspberries, Blackberries, Grapes, Etc.

PLANTS SOLD AND VARIETIES WARRANTED.

WE HAVE ALWAYS ON HAND THE NEWEST AND CHOICEST VARIETIES.

Catalogues furnished on application personally or by mail, to

A. M. PURDY, South Bend, Ind.

P. C. PERKINS,

MANUFACTURER OF

AXES & EDGE TOOLS,

ESPECIAL ATTENTION GIVEN TO

MILL PICKS AND SHINGLE KNIVES,

MISHAWAKA, IND.

ST. JOSEPH VALLEY RAILROAD

FROM WHITE PIGEON,
THROUGH
Constantine, Three Rivers & Schoolcraft,
TO
KALAMAZOO, MICHIGAN.

DAY TRAINS CONNECT WITH TRAINS EAST AND WEST ON THE MICHIGAN SOUTHERN RAILROAD AT WHITE PIGEON.

This is the important connecting Road between the Michigan Southern and Michigan Central Roads.

R. GARDNER, Supt.

HAZLITT & REED,

BOOK AND JOB

Printers,

90 WASHINGTON ST.,

CHICAGO, ILL.

Books,	*Pamphlets,*
Hand Bills,	*Business Cards,*
Billheads,	*Reports,*
Show Cards,	*Catalogues,*
Diplomas,	*Sermons,*
Programmes,	*Blanks,*

Etc. Etc. Etc.

In Good Style and at the Lowest Prices.

Estimates furnished when desired. Orders from the Country promptly attended to.

INDEX TO SOUTH BEND ADVERTISEMENTS.

INDEX TO MISHAWAKA ADVERTISEMENTS.

INDEX TO ELKHART ADVERTISEMENTS.

INDEX TO GOSHEN ADVERTISEMENTS.

INDEX TO BRISTOL ADVERTISEMENTS.

INDEX TO COLDWATER ADVERTISEMENTS.

INDEX TO MISCELLANEOUS ADVERTISEMENTS.

www.ingramcontent.com/pod-product-compliance
Lightning Source LLC
LaVergne TN
LVHW021358110826
845150LV00007B/1695

* 9 7 8 1 4 2 5 5 1 2 9 3 4 *